JAMIE PRIDE

Validate or Die

A no-nonsense, AI-powered
guide to turn bold ideas
into thriving businesses

Voices from the frontlines

'*Validate or Die* is the field manual early-stage founders have been waiting for. Jamie Pride's DreamStream Blueprint forces you to prove a problem is painful before you build, confronts the unique pitfalls facing non-technical founders, and treats founder wellbeing as a strategic asset – not a footnote. No fluff, just hard-won tactics for turning real customer pain into sustainable traction.'

Alan Jones, Partner, M8 Ventures and Top Australian Startup Mentor

'A must-read for anyone serious about building start-ups that matter, *Validate or Die* delivers an unflinching dose of truth from one of the ecosystem's sharpest minds. With a rare blend of wit, candour, and authority, Jamie challenges the fluff and inspires real action – exactly what the start-up world needs.'

Ian Mason, Former Head of Virgin Startups

'*Validate or Die* is the essential playbook for anyone seeking to turn bold ideas into commercially defensible ventures. Jamie Pride cuts through the hype, pairing frank stories of startup heartbreak with the pragmatic DreamStream Blueprint so leaders can focus on what's desirable, valuable and urgent. His AI-first lens is exactly what today's innovators need to de-risk experimentation and accelerate growth.'

Sarah Vega, National Managing Partner, KPMG Futures

'Should have been titled "Read this book or die (financially/emotionally)". Truly an insightful and helpful resource for every current and aspiring entrepreneur, from someone whose perspective can be trusted. Must read.'

Murray Hurps, Director of Entrepreneurship, UTS

'*Validate or Die* powerfully addresses the real, behind-the-scenes challenges founders face, with practical guidance on integrating AI into every validation stage. Jamie's approach transforms uncertain ideas into solid ventures that thrive in an AI-first economy.'

Charlie Wood, CEO, Wiise

'There's no denying that the arrival of AI has changed the game for startup founders. The age-old problem of how to allocate your valuable time and money needs to adjust accordingly. *Validate or Die* provides a pragmatic revision of conventional advice for this new context. Founders both new and old will benefit from updating their perspective.'

Peter Laurie, Founder at Junta and accomplished EIR

To the founders—

the restless souls who trade certainty for possibility,

who test, iterate and persist until value is born.

This book is for you.

Disclaimer

Contents

4 Forge
From prototype to product   **114**

5 Launch
Ready, set, go-live   **144**

Seizing today's AI-powered opportunities

Something has changed in me during the years since my first book, *Unicorn Tears*. I have become more convinced that we cannot simply talk broadly about product-market fit or have big visions for 'disruption'. Founders are drowning in blog posts and social media content that promise hacks, tips, and three-step formulas for success. Yet they rarely mention the mental toll behind the scenes, the sleepless nights and the spiralling fear of not keeping up with others' success stories. They also barely highlight that big leaps in tech – particularly AI – have altered the playing field for founders, especially commercial founders who do not code and have historically felt at the mercy of technical co-founders or expensive external software development agencies.

I have spent years working with startups and seen the same sorry cycle repeat: enthusiastic entrepreneurs with big ideas, genuine talent, and remarkable grit crash into the harsh reality that 'having a great idea' is no guarantee of success.

They would lose not only their money but also their confidence, their relationships, and sometimes even their sense of identity. Writing *Unicorn Tears* was my way of saying: 'We do not have to accept a 90% failure rate as inevitable.'

The startup environment has not calmed down since *Unicorn Tears* was published in 2018. If anything, it has become more crowded, frenetic, and unforgiving. At the same time, I have spent thousands of hours refining my perspective on what elements of early-stage venture building genuinely matter and which might be little more than noise. Some of my assumptions from *Unicorn Tears* have solidified the crucial role of choosing a genuine problem, the significance of building on validated user insights, and the emotional cost of drifting too far without focus. But I have also identified new accelerators that were barely on the radar in 2018, particularly the astonishing advancement of artificial intelligence tools.

I wanted to write a follow-up that would distil the timeless lessons and fresh advantages available to founders right now. So welcome to *Validate or Die: A no-nonsense, AI-powered guide to turn bold ideas into thriving businesses*. This book represents the next chapter of my conversation with all those hopeful entrepreneurs who read *Unicorn Tears* and then asked, 'What next?' If *Unicorn Tears* was about diagnosing why ventures fail, this sequel is about prescribing how to avoid those pitfalls with a sharper, more modern toolkit.

A leaner, more validated route. That is why I decided to structure this book around the essential elements I have seen matter most: precisely identifying a small, urgent segment of potential customers, validating the problem before revealing any solution, and using prototypes (not words) to prove your idea can stand on its own two feet.

I also care deeply about the concept of a founder's emotional wellbeing – because it is never just about the venture. Founders bear the perceived weight of their families' and investors' expectations, and their own sense of self-worth. Failing can *feel* devastating. Failing can *be* devastating. I want to minimise that heartache by helping you take a leaner, more validated route.

What has changed since I first wrote about these topics is how clearly I can now define the 'things that matter' in early-stage startups. For instance, founders often chase huge markets, hoping 'everyone will want this'. Yet the reality is you save your sanity by picking a **minimum viable segment (MVS)**: a small beachhead of customers who truly cannot function without your product. The founders who succeed are not necessarily the ones who attack the biggest initial market; they are often the ones who find a small segment of customers with a raw and urgent pain, deliver relief, and use that success to expand. This can often seem counterintuitive – especially when you have investors breathing down your neck for you to perform.

I have also come to see that blind problem validation – the art of investigating a user's pain without biasing them with your solution – is not just a nice step if you have time; it is *mandatory* if you want to avoid building an echo chamber around yourself. Why lead a potential customer to say, 'Yes, that sounds cool', when you can let them spontaneously admit, 'This is what I genuinely struggle with'? Many founders still skip this step – or worse, they bias the process and generate false signals. They cling to optimism rather than collecting data. It is not easy to ask direct, slightly uncomfortable questions that might prove your idea is wrong, but it is a discipline that can save you months of wasted effort and hundreds of thousands of dollars.

Equally crucial is the concept of prototype-driven solution validation. That might sound like a mouthful, but it simply means 'show, don't tell'. I have watched too many entrepreneurs try to pitch an idea in words alone, confusing potential customers because they could not truly visualise the solution. Yet a simple prototype – a clickable mock-up, a paper sketch, or a stripped-down app – reveals more than all the pitches in the world. This saves not only your resources but also your emotional bandwidth. Doing this lets you quickly learn whether users can see themselves adopting your product. If they cannot, you pivot before burning $50,000+ building the wrong solution.

We come to artificial intelligence. AI is a game-changer for startups, especially for commercial founders (founders who cannot code and develop products themselves). The ability for AI to rapidly generate designs, handle mundane tasks such as sentiment analysis of user feedback, or even help produce a functional MVP with minimal human-coding hours is enormous. AI democratises some of the labour that previously required entire development teams or a technical co-founder.

This book emphasises how AI can accelerate each step – if used thoughtfully. AI can be a double-edged sword if you rely on it blindly, but harnessing it with a clear strategy can compress timeframes, slash costs, and free your mind for the deeper, more creative aspects of founder life.

Since writing *Unicorn Tears*, I have also talked with countless commercial founders who felt disadvantaged in a tech-dominated world. 'I am not a coder,' they would lament, 'so am I doomed to rely on an expensive development agency or a mercurial CTO I can barely afford?' Today, with the proliferation and advancement of AI tools, the answer is *no*: you can prototype with no-code tools, produce brand materials with generative AI, or even build large chunks of your product's logic using accessible frameworks. This is not science fiction anymore; it is happening as we speak. So, that shift is central to the 'why' of this new book. It is not that I disregard the fundamentals of early-stage venture building – I still believe in them fiercely – but we must integrate new accelerators like AI to remain competitive.

Lastly, another shift is my clarity on who this book aims to serve. *Unicorn Tears* was my rant on why and how the startup ecosystem had lost its way. But with *Validate or Die*, I want to speak directly to a broad set of entrepreneurs. From the side-hustle dreamers who are tinkering with an idea in their spare time, to the early-stage founders who are about to embark on building their first venture, the more seasoned founders who suspect they need a sharper approach to validation, and the corporate 'escapees' who have felt locked out of the entire game. All of them share a desire to take an idea from inception and put it into the hands of customers (without causing their mental health or finances to implode).

In this book, I introduce my revised method for venture building: the **DreamStream Blueprint**. There are already many startup methods – some of which are excellent. However, with this new method, I wanted to do something different. I wanted to take out all the startup jargon. I wanted to make this new method playful and accessible.

At the same time, it is a framework grounded in real-world experience. Recently, I was voted one of the top startup mentors in Australia, and with that privilege comes a lot of face-to-face time with real founders facing very real problems. That scar tissue is baked into the DreamStream Blueprint. It is a framework that knits together the crucial steps: from that initial spark and blind validation to shaping low-fidelity prototypes, forging an initial product, and launching with real traction. I see it as a structured path that can keep founders focused on 'the next right thing' rather than drowning in confusion about product build, marketing, or user feedback.

People matter more than any single idea

I will not shy away from addressing the dark side of startup life. Reflecting on my interactions with founders of all types, I have grown increasingly aware that having the 'best' framework means nothing if the founder is crumbling under pressure. This is personal to me, not because I love talking about mental health for the sake of it, but because I have seen how ignoring it leads to burnout, broken relationships, and a sense of shame when a venture goes under. People matter more than any single idea. So, as you read about blind validation and prototypes, do not be surprised if I also remind you to check in with yourself, cultivate a support system, and avoid tying your entire identity to whether your first product launch thrives or flops.

Of course, I still believe that startups can and should aim for success beyond mere survival. I want you to build something that doesn't just limp along but thrives – where you see customers praising the difference you have made to their lives or businesses. But that success is infinitely more attainable when you focus on the few aspects that count. I have tried to peel away the fluff that confuses most founders – like chasing giant markets before securing a small beachhead or building out a 20-feature product instead of verifying that users need features 1, 2, and 3. If we accept that we can harness AI as an accelerant, the critical question becomes: which direction are we accelerating in, and why?

Sometimes, people ask me if I fear writing about such 'simple' concepts in an era that idolises unicorns: 'Isn't it way more popular to talk about hitting one billion users than building a 20-person pilot with the right niche?' After everything I have witnessed, I am more convinced that success rarely emerges from hype; it arises from consistent alignment with real user needs, from prototypes that spark immediate recognition – 'Yes, that solves my headache!' – and from doubling down on what works. Sure, some ventures skyrocket to unicorn status. Still, even then, if you dissect their earliest days, they usually started with a small test group, an unwavering focus on a specific pain, and a willingness to iterate quickly.

So this is why I wrote this book and how it links so naturally to *Unicorn Tears*. While *Unicorn Tears* addresses the heartbreak of preventable failures, this sequel is about concretely integrating AI, tight user focus, and rigorous validation into your daily routine so your idea does not just start but stays. I cannot guarantee it will be easy, but I can promise it will be better than the chaos of winging it. My aim is not to dump more theory on you but to offer a pragmatic route from 'I have an idea' to 'I have a tested product that genuinely solves something desirable, valuable, and urgent', ideally without losing your joy or your shirt.

You are not alone

If you are an early-stage founder, I hope this book reassures you that you are not alone in your fears and that there is a methodical way forward. If you are tinkering with a side-hustle idea while working full-time, I want you to see how the same strategies can protect your limited time and let you confirm viability before you leave your job. If you are more seasoned, perhaps you will find within these chapters a reminder that even with new AI possibilities, the fundamentals of validation and user-centric design remain your strongest guardrails against failure.

My cynicism for the startup sector has fluctuated heavily over the years. I have often been highly frustrated by 'wantrepreneurs', snake oil salespeople, and industry pundits. Yet, sitting down to write this book, I have a sense of hope and excitement because I genuinely believe we are in a golden age for building tested solutions faster, cheaper, and with less guesswork. Yes, the startup sector's noise level is high, which can be frustrating and even intimidating. But with the right approach – focusing on the handful of activities that matter, letting AI do some of the heavy lifting, and never losing sight of your mental wellbeing – you have an excellent chance of emerging with something that lasts. The journey may still be bumpy, but this book provides you with a map.

Welcome to *Validate or Die*. Let's get over the bullshit of fleeting, unvalidated ideas and get real – with real problems and objective data to support your solution. Let us harness the latest tools, prioritise the real user pains that cry out for attention, and design prototypes that speak louder than any pitch. Let us do all that while remembering that behind every business plan stands a person with fears, hopes, and a desire not to waste their life chasing illusions.

Enough waffle.

Let's get started.

A new blueprint for startup success

According to Microsoft more than 50 million startups are founded globally every year – an astounding figure equating to roughly 137,000 per day. If you reflect on that statistic for even a moment, it's mind-boggling. At face value, it suggests we're living in an age of boundless entrepreneurial spirit, where everyone from recent graduates to seasoned professionals can take a shot at building 'the next big thing'.

Yet, behind this optimism there's an ugly truth: around **92%** of these fledgling companies will fail within their first three years. If you were told that more than nine out of every 10 flights never reached their destination, you'd expect the entire aviation industry to halt in its tracks, meticulously investigate the causes, and enact sweeping reforms (did I mention I am afraid of flying?). But in the startup realm, these dismal figures are often shrugged off as 'just how it is', as though we should celebrate or at least accommodate this spectacular failure rate.

Why do we accept such terrible statistics so calmly?

In my experience as a founder, investor, and mentor, it's partly due to a deeply ingrained culture that romanticises risk-taking and idolises the rare success stories – the so-called unicorns. It's as though we've collectively decided that for every miraculous unicorn that emerges, it's acceptable for a thousand other ventures to tumble into obscurity, leaving behind battered founders, disenchanted investors, and a trail of wasted resources.

Why so many startups fail

When I wrote *Unicorn Tears: Why startups fail and how to avoid it*, I wanted to challenge this resigned attitude head-on. The title itself was deliberately provocative – on the one hand, we celebrate 'unicorns' (startups valued at over a billion dollars). On the other hand, we often brush aside the figurative tears shed by countless founders who pour their hearts and savings into ideas that never take flight. In that book, I argued that this failure rate is, to a large extent, preventable. Founders typically do not fail because of a single, catastrophic external event; the vast majority fail due to self-inflicted wounds – what I labelled 'internal failures'.

These internal failures range from building a product nobody truly wants to neglecting fundamental business models or succumbing to burnout and losing the drive to keep going. However, the most pervasive root cause I encountered was the lack of real validation early in the journey. Founders jumped to solutions before confirming the value or urgency of the problem, clung to half-baked assumptions, and often spent far too much time and money creating something that didn't resonate with customers.

The emotional and financial toll on founders

Let's pause to reflect on why this matters so profoundly. Much of the conversation around startup failure focuses on wasted investor money – and that's certainly a significant concern. Billions of dollars vanish every year in failed startups. However, the personal toll on founders can be even more devastating. Founders invest their time, finances, identities, reputations, and emotional energy into these ventures.

They experience:

- **Mental health pressures:** One survey found that nearly 49% of founders reported some mental health issue, whether that's depression, anxiety, or chronic stress. This number might even be conservative, as mental health remains stigmatised in many business circles.
- **Financial strain:** Many entrepreneurs, especially in early-stage tech, rely on their savings or mortgage their homes to fund that crucial first year. When the business fails, they face professional humiliation and personal economic ruin.
- **Public failure:** While failing at a large corporation might mean losing your job, startup failure happens in a glaring spotlight. Your peers, partners, family, and friends witness the collapse, often in real time. This compounds the emotional fallout.

In *Unicorn Tears*, I shared a few anecdotes and personal stories of founders who felt utterly alone in their struggles. Some had relationships on the rocks, and others turned to substance abuse. The emotional damage cannot be understated. Against this backdrop, I approach this sequel. If there's a way to alleviate even a fraction of that pain by adopting better validation techniques, stronger frameworks, and emerging technologies like AI, it's worth doing.

The 'fail fast' misconception

One of the key catalysts for this book is my ongoing frustration with how often the 'fail fast' mantra is misunderstood. The term was coined in Eric Ries's book *The Lean Startup*. Ries's concept initially encouraged founders to run quick experiments on assumptions – not to blow their entire budget on a large-scale build and then 'see what happens'. This misinterpretation is particularly dangerous for commercial founders, who can't cheaply rebuild or pivot if the concept flops.

The wrong way to look at 'failing fast':
1. Invest in a big MVP (minimum viable product) or near-finished product.
2. Launch it publicly.
3. If it fails to gain traction, treat the lost money and negative market feedback as 'just part of the journey'.

The right way to look at 'failing fast':
1. Break your hypothesis into small, testable chunks.
2. Learn from each test, refine your approach, and keep going – unless the entire concept is proven fundamentally invalid.
3. Avoid a large-scale public flop's emotional and financial drain with early identification of show-stopping flaws.

A robust validation framework – such as blind problem validation, which we'll explore later – is the buffer that helps you avoid catastrophic overspending on unverified concepts.

The latter approach is ruinous for a commercial founder whose personal funds might be at stake. **I believe most of the current startup advice and methods are built on the idea that you are a technical founder (meaning you can cut code) rather than a commercial founder.** This assumption is dangerous because it can steer commercial founders (non-technical founders) in the wrong direction. We'll examine this further throughout the book.

Commercial founders vs technical founders: the hidden divide

In the early days of Silicon Valley, the archetypal founder was technical: someone able to write code, experiment quickly, and iterate with minimal out-of-pocket expenses (think sleeping on sofas and eating ramen noodles). These founders could afford to launch half-baked products, gather real-time user feedback, and pivot within weeks. After all, the main cost was their own time and the confident drive that came with the territory. This approach shaped much of the 'startup advice' we still see today, including the notion that 'software development is cheap' or that frequent pivots cost little.

But the ecosystem has shifted since those early days. More and more founders are commercial, bringing deep industry knowledge, sales acumen, or marketing prowess but lacking coding and technical skills. For these founders, software is not 'cheap' or 'easy'. They rely on external developers, expensive agencies, or freelance talent to build basic prototypes. A single pivot can strain their budget significantly – much more so than it would a founder who can whip up a new code branch overnight.

This fundamental difference has massive implications:

- **Higher development costs:** Commercial founders might pay $50,000 (or more) to build their initial product – usually money they can't recoup if they discover, post-launch, that the problem wasn't urgent or valuable.
- **Fewer iterations:** Without in-house coding ability, each product revamp requires additional contracting or hiring (and cost), limiting how often and quickly commercial founders can pivot. This translates to fewer experiments.
- **Greater need for rigorous pre-launch validation:** Because each iteration is costly, commercial founders must get as close to the mark as possible before writing a single line of code – the first live version of the product must be 'close to the pin'. Blind validation and other development strategies become critical.

While AI is drastically bridging the gap between technical and commercial founders, there is still asymmetry. It's no longer sufficient to say, 'Just build something and see if it sticks.' For commercial founders, that attitude can lead to financial ruin. They need a robust framework that confirms a problem's urgency and a solution's viability before a chunk of their runway evaporates in development fees.

The potential hidden benefits of scarcity

If you've heard the phrase 'jack of all trades, master of none', you'll recognise the danger of dividing your focus. In the startup environment, proceeding with a lack of focus is easy: the founder who tries to tackle all sorts of customer problems simultaneously – without the money or resources to manage them – often ends up with a half-baked product that satisfies no one. I have seen this pattern of failure firsthand many times.

When you have limited resources, it forces you to make careful and deliberate choices about what truly matters. The good news is this scarcity can become a hidden advantage; however, only if you handle it properly.

Scarcity isn't just about budgets and time; it's also about your mental bandwidth. In the early days, you're likely juggling multiple roles: product manager, marketer, recruiter, counsellor to your anxious teammates, and possibly the entire engineering team if you're a solo tech founder. Multiply that by the emotional toll of not knowing whether your idea will fly and you'll see why so many well-intentioned founders burn out.

The remedy, paradoxically, is to shrink your ambition before expanding it. That doesn't mean you lose faith in the bigger dream. Instead, you focus on one clearly defined, pressing problem you can solve for a well-chosen subset of potential customers.

You might ask: 'Why aim small if I eventually want to serve millions?' The short answer is that by winning over a beachhead customer group – people who share a set of urgent pain points – you create a base that can prove your concept, generate early revenue, and be an advocate for your solution to their peers.

This **'small first'** philosophy is the core of my approach. You test each assumption in manageable steps rather than gambling everything on a big, untested hypothesis. Particularly in the initial phases, you need clarity about *who* precisely you aim to help and *why* their problem is acute.

The essential three: desirable, valuable, and urgent

Against this backdrop, I'm a massive fan of a three-pronged framework designed to ensure founders – whether commercial or technical – address their markets in a more profound, more responsible way:

- **Desirable:** Solving a problem people genuinely care about. This involves recognising that not every annoyance in life is a pressing problem, and not every problem resonates with enough customers to support a viable business.
- **Valuable:** Crafting solutions people would pay for or invest resources in. This addresses the financial viability of an idea – are you just 'interesting', or do you deliver bottom-line impact?
- **Urgent:** Ensuring there's an immediate need. Even if your product is desirable and has intrinsic value, if it's not solving a problem that users feel *right now*, it may languish on the back burner while prospective customers focus on more immediate concerns.

So, in summary: **do they want it, will they pay for it, and do they need it *now*?**

I should also point out that while you need all three elements, they are not all created equal. Most ideas I see pass the 'desirability' test. Developing a good idea that some customers will find interesting is not too difficult. **Value and urgency are a different story – and are where most founders come unstuck.** In the words of entrepreneur and educator Steve Blank, a startup is a 'temporary organisation in search of a scalable, repeatable and profitable business model'. The name of the game is profit and financial sustainability – and you cannot do that without creating something of value in the customers' eyes that they need now!

Commercial founders, in particular, must take these criteria to heart from day one. Where a technical founder might afford to 'fail fast' on a working piece of code, a commercial founder failing fast might sink tens to hundreds of thousands into a half-validated idea. That's an unsustainable dynamic.

Introducing the DreamStream Blueprint

Over many years of founding startups (with both successes and failures) and mentoring hundreds of founders, I can confidently say that success at venture building is far more science than art. Many founders get stuck in the realm of half-formed ideas and never progress to real traction. Others skip to building a prototype and discover months later that they were wrong about the customer's motivations or willingness to pay.

I have put my spin on this to capture what I believe to be the most straightforward process for starting a startup: the **DreamStream Blueprint**. Okay, okay – it's a super cheesy name, but cut me a break. I wanted something playful and accessible, and all the other good names were taken!

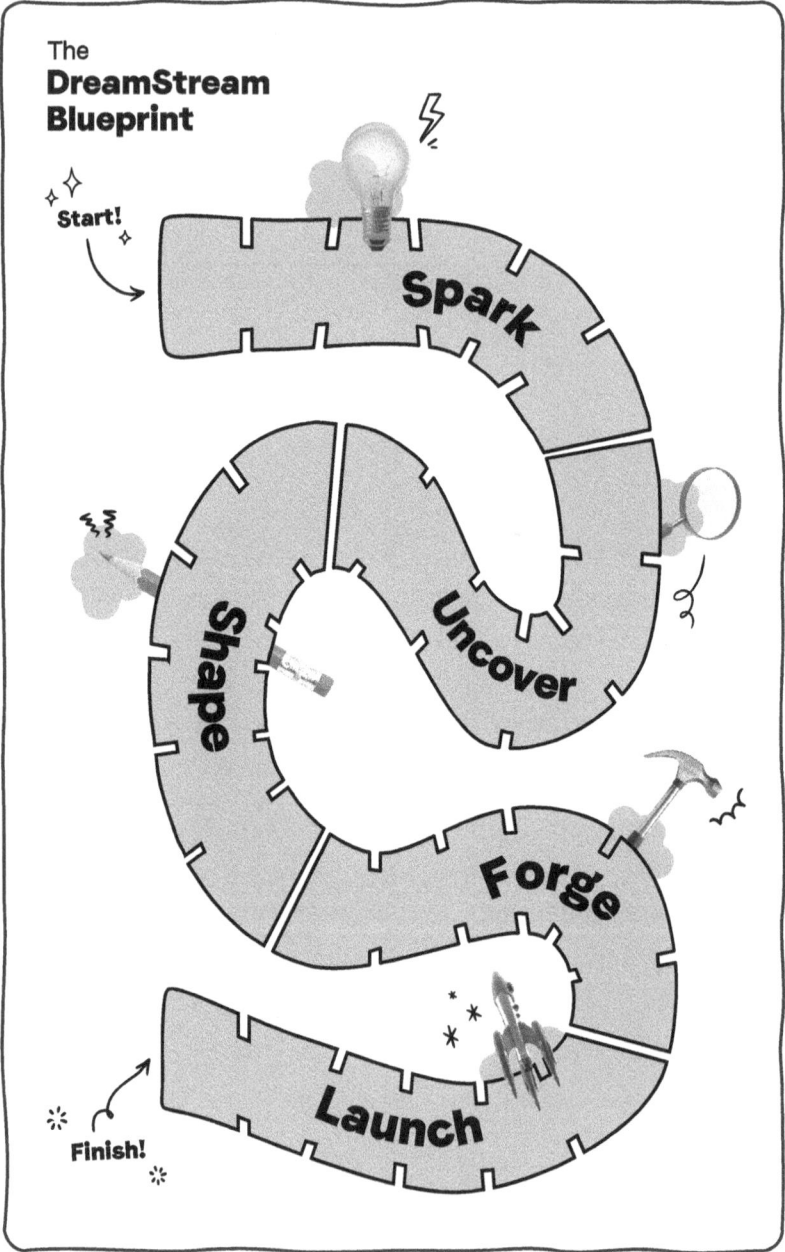

The
**DreamStream
Blueprint**

Start!

Spark

Uncover

Shape

Forge

Launch

Finish!

The **DreamStream Blueprint** is a structured roadmap that guides you from that initial spark of an idea to a live product launch, ensuring you're solving a genuine problem for a specific group of people who can't wait to adopt your solution.

At its heart, the DreamStream Blueprint comprises five phases:

1. **Spark:** You frame the opportunity and identify which people you can help first.
2. **Uncover:** You validate that these people suffer from the problem acutely without disclosing your proposed solution.
3. **Shape:** You build and test a fake version of your solution (also known as a prototype) and test that with potential users.
4. **Forge:** You turn your prototype into your launch version (also known as a minimum viable product or MVP), building out only the features your prospective customers – who now have a face and a name – desperately need.
5. **Launch:** You roll out your validated product, measure success metrics, and adapt using real-world feedback.

It sounds straightforward, but an emotional and practical rollercoaster underpins each phase. For example, the **Spark** phase is especially prone to big dreams, self-doubt, and fear of focusing on a seemingly tiny slice of the market. The temptation to chase 'everyone' from day one is strong, particularly when bullish investors or well-meaning friends ask, 'Why aim so small?' **By adopting the DreamStream approach, you channel that ambition into a step-by-step 'small-first' process that ensures you're not just building a product – you're building a product people genuinely want and are prepared to pay for.**

How this book is structured

Building a startup can feel like venturing into uncharted territory without a map. This book provides that map – a structured guide to navigating the journey from idea to market. Centred around the **DreamStream Blueprint**, the book breaks down the chaos of startup building into five clear and actionable phases. Each phase represents a crucial step in transforming a raw idea into a validated product that solves a genuine problem for real customers.

Here's how the rest of this book is organised:

1. **Spark: Igniting the idea**
   Focuses on defining the problem and identifying opportunities. Introduces the concept of a 'beachhead' or **minimum viable segment (MVS)**, helping you start small and focused while setting the groundwork for scalable success.

2. **Uncover: Validating your theory**
   Teaches blind problem validation, showing you how to gather unbiased, actionable insights from your target audience. It also discusses tools and techniques, including AI, for conducting effective user research and confirming a problem's urgency.

3. **Shape: Turning insights into solutions**
   Moves from validated insights to initial solutions. It covers creating prototypes and testing them with your prospective customers. It also emphasises starting small and iterating quickly to minimise wasted resources.

4. **Forge: From prototype to product**

   This stage guides you through turning your prototypes into a functional launch version or **minimum viable product (MVP)**. It also helps you develop your initial business model.

5. **Launch: Ready, set, go-live**

   Focuses on go-to-market strategies, acquisition experiments, and setting success metrics. It helps you achieve traction within your MVS while gathering data to adapt and grow your offering.

Each chapter stands as a guide to its respective phase, filled with practical strategies, insights, and real-world applications. Whether you're just starting or refining an existing venture, this structure allows you to focus on the areas most relevant to your current stage while keeping an eye on the bigger picture.

At the end of each chapter, you will find an exercise to help you apply what you have learnt in that chapter to the DreamStream Blueprint and to your business and product idea. This will give you a starting point for turning theory into reality. Each exercise will guide you through the key steps of that phase, helping you refine your strategy, validate your decisions, and build momentum. Whether it's mapping out your business model, stress-testing your go-to-market plan, or analysing real-world launch data, these exercises will ensure you're progressing from concept to execution.

The continued threat of unicorn tears

Why should you care about my perspective? Because I've seen the dark side of startups up close. I've felt the sting of public failure. I've experienced that sinking feeling when you realise your cash runway is burning faster than your revenue is growing. I've mentored countless founders on the brink of emotional collapse because they tied their sense of self-worth to their company's fate.

In writing this sequel, I want to shift the conversation from accepting failure as an inevitability to seeing it as largely (and possibly controversially) avoidable. Failure can mean many things, but I am referring to **catastrophic failure**, which potentially costs you everything. There is no silver bullet, but a series of best practices, mindsets, and processes that will drastically improve your odds of success. The overarching principle is that you don't have to be part of the 92% of startups that fail if you can methodically validate **desirability**, **value**, and **urgency** from the beginning – and remember to take care of your wellbeing in the process.

The **DreamStream Blueprint** is not just a framework; it's a philosophy for tackling the chaos of startup building with clarity and purpose. Breaking down the journey into structured phases gives you a roadmap to navigate the uncertainties of entrepreneurship. Each phase – Spark, Uncover, Shape, Forge, and Launch – addresses a critical aspect of turning an idea into a tangible product, reducing wasted effort and increasing the likelihood of success. But more than that, it acknowledges the human element: the emotional toll, doubts, and triumphs accompanying every founder's journey.

* * *

As we delve into the specifics of each phase, remember that this is *your* journey. The blueprint is here to guide you, but the heart of the process is your ability to adapt, learn, and persevere. Embrace the tools and insights within these pages and also embrace the unexpected lessons that will arise along the way. With focus, discipline, and the power of AI as your digital co-founder, you can navigate the complexities of building a startup, making something that truly matters to your customers and you.

CHAPTER 1

Spark ⚡
igniting the idea

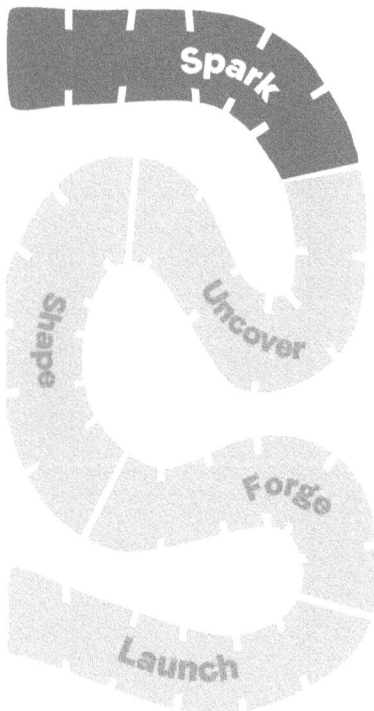

Spark	Identify the Core Problem
	Map the Market Opportunity
	Define Your Target Customer
	Analyse the Competition
	Draft Your Big Idea
	Gather Reactions and Greenlight

Uncover · Shape · Forge · Launch

Let's set the stage by clarifying what the **Spark** phase involves. In the DreamStream Blueprint, Spark consists of six key steps, as shown in the image opposite.

At first glance, these might sound straightforward – like mere checkboxes on a founder's to-do list. But they're a powerful sequence ensuring your initial vision is more than just a hunch. By following these steps, you'll build a sturdy foundation for everything that follows in your startup journey.

Let's explore the **Spark** phase.

Identifying the core problem

Every venture starts with a spark – a moment when you suddenly see an opportunity to solve something causing people genuine pain. It could be a small business owner drowning in paperwork, a student struggling with an outdated education system, or a commuter wasting hours in traffic every day. It might be a parent juggling work and childcare with no support, or a customer frustrated by clunky, inefficient technology. But before you channel your energy into building the next groundbreaking product, it's essential to ask yourself: *what exactly is the problem I'm addressing?*

When ideas first emerge, they often carry the allure of a seemingly brilliant solution. Yet, if you don't take the time to understand the true nature of the issue, you risk creating a band-aid fix rather than a lasting remedy. It's easy to become swept up in the excitement and jump straight to designing a flashy solution. However, unless you've dug deep to uncover the root cause of the pain your target audience experiences, you might spend time and resources on solution features that don't truly matter.

I like to think of it as a bit like peeling an onion. At first, you see only the outer layers – the symptoms people complain about. But if you ask yourself repeatedly, 'Why is this happening?' and you begin to peel back those layers, often what appears to be a minor inconvenience is actually a sign of a deeper, more fundamental issue. For instance, consider a company that develops a scheduling tool simply because managers complain about messy timetables. A closer look might reveal that the real problem is a rigid system that can't adapt to unpredictable demand, not simply the 'messiness'. Uncovering this underlying flaw can pivot your focus to designing a solution that offers genuine flexibility.

Engaging with your target audience

This process involves engaging directly with your target audience. Talk to people currently experiencing the problem in question; observe their day-to-day challenges, and analyse the resulting data. Whether through in-depth interviews, user journey mapping, or reviewing support queries, every piece of feedback is a clue that helps you build a complete picture. This isn't merely an academic exercise – it's about ensuring the solution you eventually develop is not just innovative but also indispensable.

One common mistake is jumping to a solution before you fully understand the problem. It's tempting to implement the first idea that comes to mind, but without a clear problem statement (discussed later), you risk creating something that only addresses the surface-level issues. Instead, take a step back and methodically validate your assumptions. Does the problem *really* keep your customers up at night? Are you addressing a recurring frustration or merely a one-off issue? Answering these questions with qualitative insights and hard data ensures you're on the right track.

Identifying the core problem is about more than listing symptoms – it's about uncovering the underlying cause that, when solved, will make a real difference. By asking the right questions and validating your findings, you conserve valuable resources and lay a robust foundation for a solution that delivers real value.

A step-by-step guide to unpacking the problem

To get to the heart of the matter, follow these steps:

1. Gather real-world insights:
- Conduct customer interviews and surveys.
- Collect data on recurring complaints.
- Observe behaviours in real-life settings (think local cafés or busy offices).

2. Analyse and prioritise:
- List all the problems mentioned by your target audience.
- Use the 'Five Whys' technique to trace each complaint to its root cause.
- Prioritise issues that occur frequently or cause significant disruption.

3. Validate assumptions with data:
- Cross-check qualitative feedback with quantitative data.
- Look for patterns in user behaviour and support requests.
- Ensure that the identified problem is not just a one-off gripe.

4. Define the problem clearly:

- Summarise the issue in a concise 'problem statement'.
- Make sure it's specific enough to guide your solution yet broad enough for future expansion.

Think of it as mapping out a complex maze: each step should lead you closer to the centre, where the true challenge lies.

Mapping the market opportunity

Before you rush headlong into validating your spark of an idea, take a moment to map the market opportunity. Why do this now? Understanding the broader industry context ensures you don't solve a problem that's too crowded with competitors or too narrow to sustain future growth.

Clarifying your market: TAM, SAM, and SOM

When you start your journey as a founder, you will be bombarded with acronyms and terms that often confuse and complicate things. Some of them are more useful than others. In terms of 'market mapping', the three you are most likely to hear about are:

- **TAM (total addressable market):** the total pool of revenue (or number of customers) that your product could theoretically serve if there were no competition and you had infinite reach
- **SAM (serviceable addressable market):** the portion of TAM that fits the constraints of your business model, geography, or product capabilities

- **SOM (serviceable obtainable market):** the realistic slice of that SAM you can target right now with your current resources. It's your near-term opportunity.

Using tools like GPT's 'Deep Research' can help you thoroughly understand these market dimensions with little effort.[1]

It's tempting to look at a giant TAM and be enticed, but the critical insight is that your immediate focus – the SOM – matters more in the early days. You can't boil the ocean. So be honest about the significance of the genuine short-term opportunity, and keep that huge TAM on the horizon as a longer-term aspiration (if ever).

One of the biggest delusions startup founders have is believing their solution has universal appeal and the world instantly needs it. Indeed, massive total addressable markets are seductive. Founders love to talk about how they only need 1% of a billion-dollar industry to become millionaires. Yet this ignores the day-to-day difficulty of acquiring customers. It's the difference between the abstract potential and persuading real people to open their wallets.

Choosing a small, urgent, well-defined segment where your idea is guaranteed to shine is essential. When you focus on a subpopulation dealing with acute pain – such as local restaurants with staff scheduling nightmares or busy working parents who can't keep up with their children's extracurricular activities – your ability to deliver desirability, value, and urgency becomes much more tangible. You can speak their language and craft a solution that immediately resonates.

---

1   OpenAI's 'Deep Research' is an AI tool that autonomously conducts in-depth research, generating cited reports, but like all AI tools currently do, it has limitations in accuracy.

The minimum viable segment

This is where a **minimum viable segment (MVS)** comes in. **The MVS – sometimes called a 'beachhead segment' – represents the smallest group of customers whose problem is so severe that they'll eagerly adopt your solution once it's available.** The term 'beachhead' comes from military strategy, referring to the initial foothold in enemy territory from which further advances can be launched. In the same way, your beachhead segment is the first wave of customers you need to win decisively. If you can succeed with them, you have a base of operations – customer testimonials, case studies, revenue – that can support later expansion into adjacent segments, or even larger new segments.

Why not just target a big market from the start? Because early-stage success doesn't typically come from a scattered approach where you attempt to woo tens of thousands of people who will all have different priorities. You'll run out of money and morale before you gain traction.

Startups operate in an environment of high uncertainty and low resources. You may have only a few months to prove traction, a small development team to build features, or a single marketing person to handle all your growth initiatives. Against this backdrop, targeting an entire market can seem overwhelming. Chasing everyone often means spreading yourself too thin – inevitably resulting in a lacklustre impact across the board.

An MVS counters this problem by forcing you to be specific. If you know you have only six months of runway, you must identify where your solution will most rapidly yield tangible results. A narrower segment with acute pain offers a more precise shot at quickly demonstrating real impact. Rather than aiming for broad recognition, seek a small group of early adopters who cannot live without the relief you offer.

Defining a minimum viable segment is one of the most strategic decisions a founder can make in the early stages of a startup. In fact, beyond value proposition, I would say it is 'the' most important decision an early-stage founder needs to make. While it can feel counterintuitive – especially amid the buzz of large TAMs, unicorn aspirations, and the cult of 'go big or go home' – focusing on a small, well-defined beachhead is often the quickest path to tangible wins. It enables you to:

- **Use resources efficiently:** Every dollar, hour, and line of code goes towards solving the most urgent pain for a clear group of users.
- **Craft targeted messaging:** By speaking directly to their challenges, your marketing will be sharper, and your conversions will increase.
- **Develop a leaner product:** You build only what your MVS needs, nothing more, accelerating your route to real feedback and revenue.
- **Establish credibility:** Early adopters become brand ambassadors, validating that your startup solves a desirable, valuable, and urgent problem.
- **Lay foundations for future growth:** Once you secure one segment, you will have the lessons and successes necessary to expand methodically.

In a founder's journey, nothing beats seeing a customer base wholeheartedly adopt your product and praise its immediate impact. By zeroing in on a single high-intensity, high-pain segment from the start, you boost the likelihood of achieving that milestone faster. From there, the rest of your market ambitions become much more attainable – stepping stones rather than leaps of faith.

So, if you're wrestling with the question of who to target first, remember: *the narrower, the better* – at least until you have a solid beachhead established. **Choose a segment with acute pain where you can deliver disproportionate value quickly and realistically grab their attention.** This isn't about curbing your ultimate vision but forging the best route to get there.

Characteristics of a good MVS

So, how do you concretely define your minimum viable segment? Well, it is more science than art. However, you may be presented with two or more equally attractive segments. If you are struggling to decide, a few key markers can guide you:

- **Acute pain:** This is the hallmark of a minimum viable segment: customers face the problem almost daily or weekly, which has a tangible negative impact on their finances, reputation, or stress levels. Are your targets facing a daily or week-to-week struggle that generates frustration or financial loss?
- **Willingness to pay:** Even if a segment's pain is intense, if they don't have the budget or purchasing authority, you risk building a solution that generates widespread desire but no conversions. This is especially important for products targeting businesses that must allocate departmental funds or get sign-off from senior leadership.
- **Easy to identify and reach:** If your targeted segment is so scattered that you can't figure out where they congregate – online or offline – it will be hard to market to them cost-effectively. You don't have an MVS if you can't find them. A well-defined MVS often shares certain channels, like

specific forums, LinkedIn groups, or industry conferences. Can you find these people in known forums, social media groups, and real-life meetups? Is there an easy way to target them with ads or direct outreach?

- **Potential evangelists:** The best MVS groups don't just buy your product – they *evangelise* it. If you win them over, they can become vocal supporters, posting case studies or sharing testimonials that help you organically expand into adjacent segments. If they love your product, will they tell their peers? Certain professions or communities share tips extensively. If your MVS is vocal, you can leverage free word-of-mouth.
- **Reasonable growth path:** While an MVS might look small initially, you should see a potential expansion path. For instance, if your beachhead is local coffee shops in one city, you might scale to coffee shops region-wide, restaurants, and other forms of hospitality once you've proven the model.

For example, if you're building an app to streamline daily tasks for busy parents, define 'busy parents' more concretely: perhaps 'working parents with children aged eight to 12 who have extracurricular activities and rely on informal carpool arrangements'. That might seem narrow, but it makes your marketing and product design precise. You can emphasise scheduling across multiple events, real-time carpool matching, or shared reminders. Parents in that scenario experience meltdown moments if a pick-up arrangement fails. That meltdown indicates a real, urgent pain.

From there, your product can expand to include older teenagers or different contexts, like group event planning for volunteer organisations. But by mastering that specific scenario, you build a solution that resonates with a slice of the market. Remember, early success stories will lay the groundwork for more significant expansions.

Why huge total addressable markets often mislead

At first glance, a pitch like, 'This is a $10 billion industry, and we only need 0.5% to become successful' appears appealing – and believe me, I have heard hundreds of these pitches. It attempts to assure investors that the opportunity is big enough.

But the nuance often missing is: how do you land that 0.5%? Where do you start, and how do you gain that initial traction? It's natural for founders – especially those seeking investor capital – to highlight how massive their total addressable market is. It reassures venture capitalists and stakeholders that a startup has room to grow. Indeed, capturing even a tiny slice of a billion-dollar market can imply huge potential revenues.

Broad, high-value markets are typically loaded with diverse customer segments with different needs. If your product aims at all of them, you perform poorly for each group, undermining your ability to scale. Potential users sense that your solution is 'okay' for them but not a standout.

However, concentrating solely on the big picture can be misleading in the early stages of a startup and may lead to such issues as:

- **Diluted focus:** Attempting to please everyone from day one usually leads to a bloated feature list, a confused product roadmap, and marketing that fails to speak compellingly to any group.

- **Longer sales cycles:** Large markets often comprise diverse user profiles and use cases. Sorting out who among them will buy immediately can be a time-consuming process – time you probably do not have if your runway is limited.
- **Inconsistent feedback:** If you're trying to serve multiple verticals or user types at once, the feedback you gather can be contradictory or irrelevant to your core assumptions.

Conversely, when you pick a smaller MVS that's part of a larger market, you have a pathway for expansion. You become the best solution for your small, urgent niche, then pivot to the next similar group, bringing real endorsements and a refined product. The large market is still out there, waiting for you to approach it with a track record of user success.

Of course, you'll eventually need to prove that you can grow. Investors may ask, 'Once you've saturated your niche, is there enough upside?' That's a fair question, but you're more likely to get funding if you show early traction than if you remain a pre-revenue entity with unproven assumptions. So, ironically, focusing on a narrower niche usually increases your odds of securing investment down the line.

The fear of focusing

One of the most significant psychological barriers to embracing an MVS approach is fear. Founders worry that by focusing on a small subset of the market they are missing out on big opportunities. Meanwhile, advisers might question whether you're thinking too narrowly. That can rattle your confidence.

Yet the emotional toll of not focusing can be worse. Imagine juggling countless feature requests and marketing messages while your runway shrinks. Stress becomes chronic, and the excitement that once fuelled you can morph into doubt or despair. Choosing an MVS is an act of self-preservation – it narrows your immediate to-do list, clarifies your message, and spares you from the heartbreak of trying to please everyone and ultimately pleasing no one.

The stress can also feel personal. If you've told friends or potential investors you'll revolutionise an entire industry, turning around to say you're focusing on a tiny slice might seem anticlimactic. But it's a short-term compromise for a long-term win. You can gently reassure family, friends, and investors that your total addressable market is still large. You're simply starting small to validate the product and build momentum.

Many successful products began by solving one specific issue for a particular customer set. Only after that customer base championed the product did the brand gain credibility and revenue to pursue a bigger audience. This pattern repeatedly emerges in startup history.

For example, Facebook initially launched as an exclusive social network for Harvard students, addressing their need for a campus-specific online community. After gaining traction within that niche, it expanded to other universities and eventually the world.

Similarly, Dropbox first targeted tech-savvy early adopters who needed a seamless way to sync and store files across multiple devices. By solving that specific problem exceptionally well, it generated word-of-mouth momentum that led to mass-market adoption.

During my time as a startup mentor, I have heard more than a few objections to this concept. Let's consider a few of the most common of these.

'But our market is huge – why limit ourselves?'
**An MVS strategy is not about limiting your ultimate market
potential. Think of it as your entry point.** Once you've
conquered one beachhead and built a sustainable base, you
can expand to neighbouring niches or more general audiences.

Apple didn't leap straight into dominating consumer electronics
across the globe. They started with hobbyist computers, then
moved into mainstream personal computing, music players,
smartphones, and more. Each success gave them credibility
and capital to tackle more significant categories, and they are
now a giant in these markets.

'We don't want to build a feature-limited product.'
It's easy to worry that you're ignoring potential features that might
appeal to other user types. But building a **minimum viable
product (MVP)** for your MVS means focusing on the must-
have capabilities that solve their most pressing pain. You can
always add more features once you confirm viability. Again, this
conserves your most precious resources of time and money.

'Investors will want to see a big TAM.'
Investors want to see big future markets but also evidence of
product-market fit. Demonstrating that you can dominate a small,
well-defined segment and show real traction often proves more
compelling than vague claims about eventually reaching tens of
millions of users.

* * *

If your MVS feels too broad, narrow it further. Instead of targeting
'independent restaurants', consider starting with 'family-owned

pizzerias in one region'. This tighter focus makes it easier to gain traction and refine your offering before expanding. Concerns about being too niche are often misplaced – early adopters understand they're part of a specialised group, and you can always reposition or rebrand as your product evolves.

As for leads outside your MVS, the decision requires careful balance. While it can be tempting to accommodate them, diverting too much attention can dilute your focus. If an outlier user fits well without straining resources, a quiet pilot could be an option – but the majority of your effort should remain on serving the core niche that will drive sustainable growth.

The power of an MVS: marketing and product focus

Having a tight group of customers to focus on will not just help with validation – it will continue to pay dividends when you need to design your product and connect with your users in the market. By understanding your MVS inside and out, you can craft bespoke messaging, product roadmaps, and go-to-market campaigns. This maximises your limited resources and ensures your first wave of users become loyal advocates, setting the foundation for future expansion.

Let's break it down.

Crafting hyper-focused messaging

The power of your MVS is best leveraged when your language resonates perfectly:

- **Use their language:** If your niche is coffee shops, you can speak about 'barista scheduling' or 'bean inventory', not 'labour management'.

- **Address specific pain:** If your customers lose an hour daily to manual data entry, your headline might read, 'Save an hour a day on manual processing'.
- **Show empathy:** With an MVS you can demonstrate that you genuinely understand their environment, limitations, and aspirations.

By tailoring your message to the specific language and experiences of your niche, you create an instant connection that builds trust and engagement.

Aligning your product roadmap

Because your MVS has well-defined pain points, you can structure your roadmap around delivering precisely what they need. Focus on core MVP features they must have, deprioritise nice-to-have add-ons, and keep a log of possible expansions once you start seeing revenue:

- **Core MVP features:** The absolute must-haves for that segment's most pressing issues.
- **Nice-to-have add-ons:** Secondary or tertiary features you might incorporate if time and budget permit (or after early adopters start paying).
- **Future expansions:** Once you've nailed the coffee shop scenario, for instance, keep a list of features or modules that would appeal to adjacent segments – like restaurants, bars, or other retail.

Focusing on the essentials ensures your product delivers immediate impact and meets the most pressing needs of your niche. With a strong foundation in place, future enhancements can be introduced strategically, driven by user feedback and revenue growth.

Targeted go-to-market campaigns

When you know your MVS intimately, you can tailor your go-to-market (GTM) approach. Choose channels that speak directly to them, such as niche online forums, mini-events, or micro-influencers. Avoiding broad or generic marketing will stretch your limited budget and generate better conversion rates:

- **Select the right channels:** If your beachhead is indie game developers, maybe X and Discord communities yield better ROI than LinkedIn.
- **Micro-influencers and thought leaders:** Identify individuals who speak specifically to your segment's pain and partner with them for webinars, blog posts, or co-branded content.
- **Local or niche events:** Instead of paying top dollar for a big industry expo, sponsor a small, sector-specific conference your MVS is likely to attend.

This hyper-focused GTM strategy saves money and yields better leads and faster conversions because you only show up where your MVS truly congregates, based on research and not wild guesses.

Expanding beyond your MVS

How do you know when to expand beyond your beachhead?

That question is best answered when you have achieved significant segment penetration or see apparent parallels with other customer groups. If your product is an invoicing system and your MVS is 'independent design freelancers', the next segment might be 'independent photographers' because perhaps they share similar invoicing routines. Over time, you can scale from single usage to multi-user teams or shift from freelancers to boutique agencies and eventually target entire corporate departments if your product truly excels.

When to expand

It's tempting to jump to the next segment as soon as you have a handful of paying users. But expanding too early – before achieving solid product fit in your MVS – can spread your resources too thin and dilute your focus. **To maximise your chances of long-term success, first establish clear traction within your initial niche.**

For a business offering, that means 100+ paying customers who actively use and rely on your product. This ensures that your solution isn't just being trialled but is truly solving a problem at scale within that segment.

For a consumer product, the threshold is typically much higher. Depending on the industry, you may need 1000 to 10,000+ paying customers to confirm sustainable demand. Consumer markets often require greater volume due to lower average revenue per user and higher churn rates. Before expanding to new audiences, you should see strong retention, repeat purchases (if applicable), and a growing base of organic referrals – signs that your product is truly resonating.

Jumping into a broader market before securing your foundation can lead to wasted marketing spend, increased churn, and a lack of clarity on what's actually working. Stay disciplined, refine your core offering, and expand only when the data proves it's time.

If you are tempted, consider:

- **Market saturation:** Have you penetrated a significant slice of your MVS? There may still be plenty more similar users you haven't reached.

- **Stability and feedback:** Ensure your product is stable, user feedback is mostly positive, and you've refined your core features.
- **Revenue confidence:** If you rely on revenue to sustain development, wait until your MVS produces enough consistent cashflow – or until you've secured investor interest.

Identifying adjacent markets

Adjacent expansions can be geographical (for example, from city-level coffee shops to state-level ones), vertical (for example, from coffee shops to juice bars), or feature-based (for example, adding inventory management so you can also serve small convenience stores).

Here's what you should aim to do with your expansions:

- **Leverage existing features:** This minimises the additional engineering or marketing overhead required.
- **Share pain points:** The new segment's challenges should be similar enough that your current solution remains relevant.
- **Build on past success:** Testimonials and case studies from your MVS should easily translate to the new group's context.

Avoiding the 'one-size-fits-all' trap

Just because you've succeeded with one segment doesn't mean you can claim to serve 'all' of hospitality or 'all' scheduling or invoicing needs. Each new market will require tailored messaging, slight feature adjustments, or custom integrations. **Resist the urge to brand yourself as the universal solution too quickly, or you might lose the clarity and focus that made you successful.**

MVS as a foundational mindset

Defining the MVS isn't just a marketing exercise; it's a lifeline for founders drowning in uncertainty. Once you articulate precisely who you're serving, your decisions about feature prioritisation, messaging, and branding become clearer. You're no longer building for 'everyone who has trouble keeping track of finances' but rather 'independent freelancers in design agencies who struggle with invoicing at the end of each month'.

When you refine your MVS to that level of specificity, your product roadmap can zero in on precisely what freelancers need – perhaps automated invoice reminders, integration with commonly used design tools, or templates for repeat clients. This depth spares you from feature bloat and resonates with users who will feel heard and understood.

It's natural to fear that you might be excluding other potential users. For instance, what if a mid-sized accounting firm is interested in your invoicing solution? You can allow them to sign up if they demonstrate interest. The key difference is that you aren't yet committing your main marketing or development resources to that larger group. Your primary focus remains on perfecting the experience for the freelancers who embody your MVS.

An MVS strategy isn't merely a box to check; it's a guiding principle that can influence every dimension of your startup:

- **Product philosophy:** Even when you do expand, you can treat each new segment as its own MVS. Develop the habit of profoundly understanding each user group and customising the product to fit their top concerns first.

- **Hiring and team culture:** A small, specialised user base means your support and marketing teams develop deep empathy. They learn to speak your users' language, enabling more genuine relationships. When you scale, that customer-centric ethos can permeate the organisation.
- **Ongoing validation:** As blind and prototype-driven validation continues throughout your product's lifecycle, so does MVS thinking. If you're adding a new feature or pivoting, ask yourself: *which sub-segment experiences the greatest need for this?* That question ensures you keep shipping 'must-have' updates rather than superfluous ones.

Analysing the competition

Understanding your competitors isn't about copying what others do – it's about 'positioning'. I will mention this concept several times in this book because it is important. Positioning is, however, so often underrated and underutilised as a strategy by founders.

Identifying which segment of the market your competitors are targeting and how they do it is essential. Specifically, how are they positioning themselves? Before you position your product in the market, take a moment to assess the landscape. This process extends beyond counting features and pricing; it involves exploring the strategies, strengths, and weaknesses of those already competing for the same customers.

Imagine you're developing a new invoicing solution. A glance at the market might reveal several players offering similar services. By analysing their offerings in detail, you might notice that some are feature-rich and focused on 'big business' or enterprise clients, while others may be focused on verticals such as tradies. This realisation can inspire you to position yourself in different ways – be it price or product.

To begin this analysis, gather as much publicly available information as you can. Explore competitor websites, review platforms, and customer forums. Consider:

- Where do their solutions fall short?
- What problems are their clients still facing?

You'll often find that a product which seems robust on paper may not perform as expected in practical, everyday use. These gaps present opportunities for you.

It's also worth considering how competitors communicate their value. Is their message clear, or do they leave potential customers with unanswered questions? The language they use often reveals a lot about their understanding of both their own product and their market. When you spot inconsistencies or vague promises, you've likely uncovered an area where your approach can be sharper and more direct.

Ultimately, analysing the competition is about arming yourself with the knowledge needed to discover your niche. It transforms the crowded market into a series of opportunities waiting to be seized, enabling you to build a product that isn't just another option but the definitive solution for your target audience.

How to analyse your competitors: a quick guide

Understanding your competitors is essential for refining your strategy and carving out a competitive edge. A well-structured analysis helps you uncover their strengths, weaknesses, and positioning in the market. This quick guide breaks down the key steps to gathering insights that will inform your product development and differentiation.

1. **Gather data:**
   - Research competitor websites, customer reviews, and social media channels.
   - Compile key details on product features, pricing, and customer support.

2. **Identify strengths and weaknesses:**
   - Note what competitors do well – such as intuitive design or strong after-sales service.
   - Highlight gaps where customer needs remain unmet.

3. **Assess market positioning:**
   - Evaluate how they communicate their value proposition.
   - Determine if their messaging is clear and compelling.

4. **Benchmark performance:**
   - Compare user experience, product reliability, and customer satisfaction metrics.
   - Look for trends in market feedback and recurring complaints.

5. **Extract opportunities:**
   - Identify areas where you can offer a distinctive advantage.
   - Focus on improving aspects that competitors consistently overlook.

By following these steps, you will equip yourself with actionable insights that inform your product strategy. This structured approach will highlight where your competitors fall short and point to opportunities where your solution can truly stand out.

Coping with founder stress in the Spark stage

No founder is immune to the emotional highs and lows of this journey. On the one hand, you're itching to do everything at once – massive PR campaigns, big partnership deals, multi-feature product roadmaps. On the other hand, you might be petrified that focusing on a small segment could leave you looking unimpressive or lead you to a dead end if your chosen MVS doesn't pan out.

Yet it's precisely this tension that the Spark phase addresses. By stepping back to define a small but potent group of customers you're creating a safer environment to test your assumptions. If your concept proves correct, you'll see tangible signs of progress: a cluster of customers deeply grateful for your solution, early revenue that keeps your lights on, and maybe even inbound inquiries from neighbouring niches. That kind of traction ignites confidence in you and your investors.

Imagine a founder who's never hammered out the specifics of their MVS. They might launch a 'productivity app for everyone', invest many thousands in ads that target broad demographics, and get a trickle of sign-ups from random user segments. Sure, a couple of them might stick around, but there's no coherence in how they use the app or how to evolve the features. The founder's time is spent firefighting: chasing partial leads, building half-hearted features, and wrestling with contradictory feedback.

Contrast that with the founder who says, 'We build a scheduling tool specifically for independent hair salons with part-time stylists.' It sounds limiting, but the product can deliver immense value within that niche. Salons can quickly see whether the tool reduces scheduling confusion, cuts no-show rates, or increases stylist utilisation. If successful, other salons take note, and the founder can later pivot to larger establishments. That sense of clarity also keeps the founder's anxiety in check. They know where to focus their next feature cycle. They know how to speak in a language that resonates with hair salon owners. And when they approach each prospective customer, they can say, 'We've done this for three other hair salons – here are their results.'

Transitioning to Uncover

Having defined your MVS in principle, the real question now becomes: how do you verify that these people genuinely suffer from the problem you're so keen to solve? It's easy to speculate that coffee shop owners or freelance designers experience daily pain. Confirming it through genuine conversations that aren't skewed by your solution pitch is another matter entirely.

That's the job of the next phase in the DreamStream Blueprint: **Uncover**. In Uncover, you'll delve into blind problem validation, digging deep into your target customers' experiences without giving away your big idea. This ensures you're not just hearing polite niceties or going down a solution-biased path. By the end of Uncover, you'll emerge with unambiguous proof that your chosen beachhead is indeed standing on a burning platform and needs a lifeline. Or, if the feedback suggests otherwise, you'll pivot before you blow your precious resources on a fantasy.

Such is the beauty of taking it step by step. Spark helps you see the power of picking a small, urgent segment. Then,

Uncover ensures that this segment's urgency is real, not just an assumption. With those insights, you'll be ready to shape the precise offering that meets them where they are, forging early prototypes with confidence rather than guesswork.

So, if you are anxious about going small, remember (cliché alert): a tiny spark can turn into a roaring fire if you gather the right fuel. The MVS is that concentrated fuel source – enough to ignite your startup in the short term and a stepping stone towards capturing a greater market share once you've proven you can deliver real impact.

Take heart in the knowledge that you're not limiting your ultimate dream. You're simply acknowledging that every journey worth taking begins with a single step. And this single step, the Spark stage, sets the tone for everything that follows. Your startup's future expansions and successes will be far more solid and credible when they emerge from the foundation you build right here.

Prepare to step beyond the comfort of your ideas and into the real world of customer interviews, emotional baggage, and honest, unfiltered feedback. Remember, confronting reality early doesn't dampen your ambition – it refines it, ensuring the idea doesn't flicker out due to your biases, beliefs, and bullshit. It's time to face your chosen beachhead head-on, equipped with empathy, curiosity, and determination to confirm you truly need what you're about to build.

Top five Spark tips to remember

These top five tips from **Spark** will keep you focused, strategic, and on the path to sustainable growth. By starting with a narrow, well-defined niche, validating your positioning, and resisting the urge to expand too soon, you set yourself up for long-term success. Nail one market first – then scale with confidence:

1. **Start small but intentional:** Don't let the allure of massive markets fool you – focus on the smallest possible segment that is experiencing acute pain.
2. **Map before you validate:** Use tools like TAM, SAM, and SOM and a competitor assessment to grasp where you really fit.
3. **Speak to their pain:** Hyper-focus your marketing on your target users' specific language, frustrations, and needs.
4. **Stay calm amid FOMO:** The fear of missing out on bigger markets is natural. Refine your MVS to protect yourself from chaos and wasted resources.
5. **Treat expansion as a future reward:** Prove success in one segment first, gather momentum, and then spread your wings with confidence.

The DreamStream Blueprint: Spark

Now that we've explored the Spark phase in depth, it's time to put these principles into action. The six Spark steps in the DreamStream Blueprint – Identify the Core Problem, Map the Market Opportunity, Define Your Target Customer, Analyse the Competition, Draft Your Big Idea, and Gather Reactions and Greenlight – form a structured approach to refining your startup concept. Let's work through each step so you can apply them to your own idea.

1. Identify the core problem

What's keeping your potential customers up at night?

- Start with broad observations, then dig deeper using the 'Five Whys' technique.
- Speak to real potential customers – what's frustrating them daily, and why?
- Differentiate between surface symptoms and root causes.
- Frame your problem statement clearly: *If we solve X, it will fundamentally improve Y.*

Action step: Write a concise problem statement that summarises the core frustration your product will resolve.

2. Map the market opportunity

How big is the market, and where do you fit'?

- Use TAM, SAM, and SOM to assess the market's true potential.
- Identify trends and shifts – why is this the right time for your idea?
- Pinpoint gaps where competitors aren't fully addressing customer pain.

Action step: Estimate the size of your SOM (serviceable obtainable market) and describe how your idea will capture it.

3. Define your target customer

Who needs this solution most, right now?

- Narrow your focus to your minimum viable segment (MVS).
- Define key traits – industry, role, income level, painpoints, and existing behaviours.
- Consider psychographics: what motivates them, what are their biggest frustrations, and what solutions have they already tried?

Action step: Write a profile of your ideal early adopter, including their biggest challenge and why they would switch to your solution.

4. Analyse the competition

What's already out there, and how can you stand out?

- List your direct and indirect competitors.
- Identify their strengths and weaknesses.
- Spot positioning opportunities – what can you do differently or better?

Action step: Create a simple competitor comparison table highlighting where your solution outperforms existing options.

5. Draft your big idea

What's your unique approach to solving the problem?

- Develop a clear and simple one-liner explaining your idea.
- Describe what makes your solution different, better, or more compelling.

- Consider pricing, features, and business model –
  how will you sustain growth?

Action step: Write your 'elevator pitch' – a two-sentence
summary of your startup that clearly states the problem,
your solution, and why it matters.

6. Gather reactions and greenlight

Are you on the right track, and do people care?

- Test your idea with real potential customers –
  gather feedback before building anything.
- Use surveys, interviews, and landing pages to
  gauge interest.
- Look for strong signals – are people excited?
  Would they pay for it?

Action step: Outline your plan for gathering feedback –
who will you talk to, what will you ask, and how will you
measure responses?

REFLECT AND ADAPT

Once you've worked through these six steps, take a step back and evaluate:

- What assumptions were challenged or disproven?
- Where did you uncover unexpected insights?
- Do you need to refine your problem statement, target market, or core offering?

This isn't a one-and-done process – iterate as you learn. By rigorously applying these steps, you'll set the stage for a startup idea that isn't just exciting on paper but has real market potential. Now, with a validated concept in hand, it's time to move to the next phase: **Uncover**.

NOTES

CHAPTER 2

Uncover
validating your theory

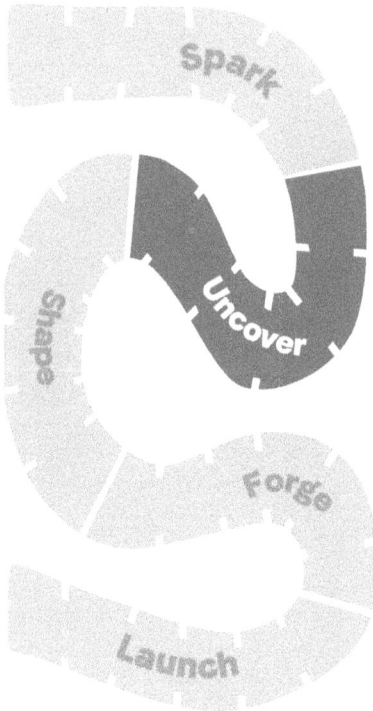

Spark

Uncover

Shape

Forge

Launch

Clarify Your Assumptions

Map the Customer Journey

Design Your Interview Questions

Recruit Interview Participants

Conduct Problem Interviews

Weigh Risks and Decide

ompleting the foundational steps in the **Spark** phase, from identifying your minimum viable segment to clarifying the market opportunity, laid the groundwork. In the **Uncover** phase, we'll take a microscope to real customer problems, ensuring we are not just chasing wishful thinking. And if there's one thing I've learned, it's this: the best ideas stand on the shoulders of genuine customer data and insights, not assumptions.

Consider the feeling of holding a key in your hand but not yet knowing which door it opens. You sense its importance – solid, tangible, and full of potential. Yet, its actual value remains uncertain until you find the right lock. This is precisely where many founders find themselves after identifying a potential minimum viable segment (MVS). They have a promising lead, but they've yet to confirm whether it will unlock the burning, urgent, valuable pain their target customers genuinely experience.

That uncertainty might keep you awake at night, your mind churning with questions. *What if I'm chasing a phantom problem? What if my beachhead doesn't care?* This anxiety is perfectly normal. In fact, it's healthy. It prompts you to gather genuine evidence before you invest the next six months in building a product that only exists in your imagination.

I call this phase **Uncover** because it involves unearthing raw, unfiltered truths about your potential customers, their struggles, and how they affect them daily. In the DreamStream Blueprint, Uncover means systematically confirming that your MVS is genuinely grappling with the problem you want to solve – is it desirable, valuable, and urgent? You do this through blind problem validation, a series of customer interviews or conversations that focus squarely on their pain, not your presumed solution.

Start with the customer journey

Before diving into validation, it's helpful to visualise how your potential customers interact with the relevant problem in their daily routines. Think of it as building a simple storyboard of your user's day: *where does the frustration first appear? When is it worst? Where does it taper off?*

Here are some things to consider:

- **Identify key touchpoints:** These are the moments or activities where a customer encounters obstacles or inefficiencies.
- **Pinpoint emotional highs and lows:** Do they describe a particular step as 'soul-sucking' or 'tedious'? These emotional triggers signal the hottest pain points.
- **Capture context:** Who else is involved at each step? What external factors – like time pressures, budget constraints, or staff limitations – magnify the issue?
- **Summarise the journey:** A simple flowchart or timeline can help you see patterns, revealing exactly where your potential solution might fit.

Mapping the customer journey ensures you're not just hearing about *what* the user's pain is – you're also seeing *where* and *when* it hurts the most. This holistic view forms a robust foundation for subsequent interviews and helps you avoid focusing on symptoms while missing the root problem.

Be problem-oriented rather than solution-oriented

One of the most defining traits of successful founders is their orientation – whether they are problem-oriented or solution-oriented. At first glance, solution-oriented founders might appear more desirable. They are the ones who come armed with a bold idea or a shiny prototype, ready to dazzle the world. Yet, despite the allure of having 'the perfect solution', solution-oriented founders often find themselves blindsided by the harsh realities of the market. In contrast, problem-oriented founders – those who dedicate themselves to profoundly understanding a customer's pain before offering a fix – consistently outperform their solution-driven peers. Why is that?

Developing a deeper customer understanding

Problem-oriented founders see their role not as saviours with a ready-made answer but as detectives uncovering the intricate web of their customers' struggles. They start with questions, not assertions. Instead of rushing to declare, 'This is what you need', they ask, 'What is causing this frustration? What impact does it have on your day-to-day life? Why hasn't it been solved before?' This relentless curiosity does more than uncover the surface-level symptoms of a problem; it reveals the underlying drivers that must be addressed to create a truly effective solution.

For example, consider a founder targeting small retailers struggling with stock reconciliation. A solution-oriented founder might leap to build an AI-powered inventory tracker, assuming it's the answer. However, a problem-oriented founder would take the time to interview those retailers, discovering that reconciliation is time-consuming and that outdated hardware, lack of staff training, and irregular supplier deliveries compound the issue. With this deeper understanding, the problem-oriented founder can design a solution addressing reconciliation and the broader inefficiencies causing the pain.

Iteration as a superpower

Another key strength of problem-oriented founders is their flexibility. Because they don't tie their identity to a specific solution, they are far more willing to pivot or iterate when the feedback indicates their initial approach isn't working. They view their solution as a hypothesis – something to test and refine – rather than a fixed answer they must defend at all costs.

Solution-oriented founders, by contrast, often fall into the trap of 'falling in love' with their idea. This attachment can cloud their judgement, leading them to ignore or dismiss critical feedback that contradicts their assumptions. They might double down on an approach clearly not resonating, pouring time and resources into a solution fundamentally misaligned with customer needs. It's a classic case of driving straight off a cliff, Thelma-and-Louise style, rather than course-correcting to find a safer route.

The feedback advantage

Problem-oriented founders are inherently better equipped to leverage feedback. They listen without defensiveness because they are not married to a specific solution. When a customer says, 'This doesn't solve my problem', they lean in and ask, 'Why? What's missing? What would make it better?' This mindset creates a feedback loop that drives continuous improvement, allowing their product to evolve in ways directly informed by real customer pain.

Solution-oriented founders, on the other hand, often interpret feedback as criticism of their idea. This can lead to defensiveness or outright denial – 'The customer just doesn't get it' – rather than the introspection needed to make meaningful changes. The result is often a stubborn refusal to iterate, leaving them vulnerable to more responsive and adaptive competitors.

Lowering the stakes

Problem-oriented founders also benefit from a psychological advantage: they don't see a failed solution as a personal failure. Because their identity is tied to solving the customer's problem – not a specific solution – they are less emotionally crushed when an approach doesn't work. This resilience allows them to pivot quickly, try new methods, and keep moving forward.

In contrast, solution-oriented founders often tie their self-worth to the success of their idea. When that idea falters, the emotional toll can be crippling, leading to burnout or a complete abandonment of the venture. By focusing on the problem rather than the solution, problem-oriented founders stay grounded in their mission, even as they adapt their tactics.

The market rewards problem solvers

The market consistently rewards founders who approach their work with a problem-first mentality. Customers don't care how clever your solution is; they care whether it alleviates their pain. Investors, too, are more likely to back founders who demonstrate a deep understanding of their target audience's struggles, as this understanding is the foundation of long-term success.

A flashy solution might generate initial excitement, but a solution rooted in genuine customer insight creates lasting value.

The mindset shift

Shifting from a solution-oriented to a problem-oriented mindset requires humility. It means accepting that your initial idea might be wrong – or, at the very least, incomplete. It means prioritising discovery over certainty and curiosity over conviction. But for founders willing to make this shift, the rewards are immense: greater clarity, stronger user engagement, and a product that truly addresses the needs of its market.

Ultimately, being problem-oriented is not just about strategy but also philosophy. It's about recognising that your ultimate job as a founder is not to impose your vision on the world but to co-create solutions with your customers grounded in their lived realities. It's a mindset that doesn't just lead to better products – it leads to better founders.

Biases, beliefs, and bullshit redux

In the current startup environment, there's a powerful temptation to shout your idea from the rooftops. After all, you're excited and would love to rally early support. However, this eagerness can inadvertently sabotage your fact-finding mission. **There is a brief but critical 'golden window' during problem validation when your proposed solution hasn't coloured the customer's perception.** In that window, you can uncover the most genuine account of their challenges: the actual depth, frequency, and emotional toll of the problem they face.

The second you 'unblind' them and describe your brilliant concept – whether it's an app, a platform, or a hardware device – you change the dynamics of the conversation. People may say they love it (either out of politeness or genuine curiosity), or they may raise objections that only pertain to the specific way you've framed your solution. In either case, you lose the chance to see if the underlying concept resonates with them on its merit.

Courtesy bias is also a major risk in early validation interviews – if you pitch your idea too eagerly, people may nod along out of politeness rather than genuine interest. Blind problem validation avoids this by keeping your solution hidden and focusing instead on their experiences: how often they feel the pain, how they cope, and what it costs them. This aligns with Rob Fitzpatrick's *The Mom Test*, which emphasises unbiased questioning. Instead of asking, 'Would you use an app that does X?' – which invites empty enthusiasm – ask, 'How do you currently handle this problem, and what's the hardest part?' Shifting the focus from your idea to their reality reveals true demand.

This is why blind problem validation is so critical. Blind validation is a product testing method where participants contribute without knowing key details such as the brand, specific features, or expected performance. This ensures their feedback is based purely on their existing needs and experience rather than preconceived opinions or brand loyalty. (In some cases, even the researchers conducting the evaluation are 'blind', meaning they do not know which product variation they are assessing, further eliminating bias.)

By removing your solution from the picture, you focus entirely on understanding your potential customers' frustrations, needs, and desires. **This unbiased perspective ensures you're solving a problem that genuinely matters – not just one you assume exists.** If your discussions confirm that the pain is real, you can proceed to test your solution with greater confidence. If not, you've spared yourself wasted resources and emotional anguish.

Flawed validation is worse than no validation

Many founders believe they've validated their problem when, in fact, they've fallen into the trap of flawed or biased validation. This is not just unhelpful – it's outright dangerous. It creates false signals that lead to a false sense of security, resulting in startups being built on what is essentially a house of cards.

When I ask founders, 'Have you validated your problem?' the response is almost always an enthusiastic *yes*. But dig deeper, and you'll find that their validation was riddled with confirmation or courtesy bias. They pitched their solution upfront, received a few polite nods or compliments, and walked away believing they had uncovered genuine demand. In reality, they hadn't tested the problem: they had tested their ability to elicit politeness.

Startups built on flawed validation are incredibly fragile. A single gust of real-world feedback can send the entire structure tumbling down. Why? Because the false sense of security blinds founders to early warning signs. They become so invested in their perceived validation that they ignore evidence contradicting their assumptions. Painfully, the first time these founders receive real validation is on product launch – after spending a lot of time, resources, and dollars building a product – and they are often shocked to discover no one wants to buy it and they now have limited cash runway to recover.

Why commercial founders in particular must validate properly

For founders who can code their prototypes cheaply, skipping blind validation might not be as financially lethal. They can afford to build a rudimentary product, launch quickly, and gauge market reaction. However, for commercial founders, each line of code likely carries a hefty price tag. Hiring a developer or outsourcing an app build can run into tens or hundreds of thousands before you even know if the problem is worth solving. Even with advances in AI app generation there is still a cost to develop – be it money or time.

That's precisely why blind validation is even more critical for commercial founders. By thoroughly confirming the market's pain point at a low cost – through interviews, surveys, or AI-driven sentiment analysis – you minimise the risk of pouring hard cash into building the wrong solution. Pivoting after an expensive MVP is a luxury many commercial founders do not have.

Imagine you're a sales executive with a strong network in the retail industry. You suspect retailers struggle with real-time inventory tracking. You could spend $30,000 to $50,000 to hire a freelance team to build a minimal product that seeks to solve that problem. But what if, after launch, you learn that retailers find their current solutions adequate – or that their real pain lies in something else entirely, like labour management? Blind validation could have surfaced that insight through a few weeks of interviews and desk research, costing only a fraction of what you'd otherwise commit to development.

How to conduct a successful blind validation process

Let's break down blind validation into its components, providing a guide for those ready to implement it. I've also included a framework to assist you in putting it into practice, helping you integrate blind validation effectively into your workflow.

Define the problem

You begin by articulating in general terms the type of pain you believe people might have. For instance, if you suspect small retailers struggle with end-of-day stock reconciliation, phrase it neutrally: 'Many small shops face time-consuming tasks after closing hours.' Avoid describing your proposed solution ('an AI-powered inventory scanner') at this stage – your goal is to confirm the *problem*, not sell a *solution*.

Find the right people

Blind validation means little if you're speaking to the wrong people. Identify the customer profile most likely to experience your outlined pain – this should be your minimum viable segment (MVS). Review the profile you developed for your MVS in the Spark phase. Now is the time to refine and tighten it up and put it to good use.

Establish target selection criteria

Once you are happy with the MVS you want to explore, define criteria to help you choose **20 potential interviewees**. For example, if you focus on retailers, you might specify additional criteria beyond the MVS if needed, such as:

- at least two years in business
- revenue above (or below) a certain threshold
- specific industry sub-verticals (for example, clothing shops vs health stores).

By outlining these additional criteria, you can ensure the people you speak with are relevant.

Identify 20 target customers

Aim for a manageable total of 20 individuals or organisations to interview about their problem. Depending on your industry, these could be business owners, end-users, department heads, or influencers who face (or witness) the pain you believe exists. If your problem space has several different stakeholders (such as a two-sided market), I suggest leaning towards interviewing people who will pay for your solution. Remember that scheduling and conducting interviews is often more time-intensive than you'd think, so choose your 20 carefully.

Prioritise and group targets (Friendlies, Contenders, Prospects and Whales)

Rather than rushing all 20 problem interviews, consider grouping them into four groups of five:

- **Friendlies:** People you already know or have a casual relationship with. Interview these people or organisations first. They're lower risk and provide good 'practice' interviews while you refine your approach.
- **Contenders:** Contacts in your broader network or industry peers who are more neutral. They'll be honest, but they're not yet your highest-stakes conversations.

- **Prospects:** Individuals who closely resemble your intended user or customer and whose feedback will validate the problem's commercial feasibility.
- **Whales:** The highest-value, most influential interviews. These could be industry leaders, big customers with multi-location operations, or highly respected thought leaders. Conduct these interviews last, when you will be best prepared and have the most information.

This progression allows you to **refine your interviewing skills** with 'Friendlies' first. After every five interviews, take time to reflect on what you've learned. You may need to update your question set or resequence your questions. By the time you reach your 'Whales', you'll be well-practised, ensuring that every minute of their time provides maximum insight.

Craft open-ended questions

When conducting blind validation interviews, how you frame your questions can be the difference between uncovering genuine insights and inadvertently confirming your biases. Rob Fitzpatrick's *The Mom Test* is a fantastic guide to this process, stressing that you should **avoid pitching your idea** or asking hypothetical questions. Instead, focus on how people behave and how they've handled similar problems recently.

Below are a few pointers drawn from *The Mom Test*, along with ways AI can help:

Ask about actual behaviour, not opinions

Pitfall: 'Would you pay for a solution like mine?'

Better: 'When was the last time you encountered [problem], and how did you deal with it?'

Focusing on actual events rather than hypothetical futures will reveal the problem's true importance and whether people are motivated enough to spend money or effort to solve it.

Dig into past and present frustrations

Pitfall: 'Do you think [problem] might matter to you next year?'

Better: 'What's the most recent example of [problem] causing you an issue, and how often does that happen?'

This line of questioning helps you gauge the frequency and emotional toll of the issue. If someone struggles with the problem daily or weekly, it's likely urgent. However, if they can't recall the last time it happened, you may be chasing a non-issue.

Focus on specific incidents and numbers

Pitfall: 'Do you see this as a big or small issue?'

Better: 'How many hours a week do you spend on [task], and what's the cost (financial or emotional) of dealing with it?'

Press for concrete details – time, money, human resources, or stress-level metrics. This reveals the genuine magnitude of the problem.

Resist hypothetical or leading questions

Pitfall: 'If I built an AI tool, would you use it?'

Better: 'How are you currently solving [problem], and what do you like or dislike about those methods?'

Leading questions often yield biased responses, especially if interviewees sense you're fishing for compliments or validation.

A step-by-step interview framework

Here's a concise framework covering who to interview, what to ask, and common pitfalls to avoid – helping you uncover real insights about the problem you're solving. By structuring your approach, you can identify true pain points, filter out misleading feedback, and avoid the trap of hearing what you want to hear instead of what's actually there. Follow these steps to ensure your conversations provide actionable data rather than empty validation.

1. Plan your recruiting strategy:

- **Define clear personas:** Pin down exactly who suffers from the problem (age, role, business size).
- **Leverage existing networks:** Start with Friendlies, but don't stay there. Expand to relevant industry contacts or LinkedIn groups.
- **Offer a reciprocity hook:** People are likelier to say yes if they see a benefit – like a future whitepaper, early access, or a small-dollar gift card.

2. Prepare your interview template:

- **Open with context:** Briefly explain why you're researching this problem *without mentioning your solution.*
- **Use open-ended questions:** Focus on actual behaviours, frequency of the pain, and emotional toll.
- **Keep it short:** Aim for 20 to 30 minutes. Asking for extended interviews will deter participants – and the interviews will exhaust you!

3. Conduct the interview:

- **Listen actively:** Let them speak without interruption. Take notes on specific words, body language, and emotional cues.

- **Probe for detail:** Ask follow-up questions ('When exactly does this happen?').
- **Resist pitching:** Avoid revealing your concept or saying, 'I'm building X to fix that!'

4. Document and reflect:

- **Accurately capture key quotes:** Verbatim statements can be revealing.
- **Look for patterns:** Do multiple interviewees share the same frustrations?
- **Note conflicting insights:** Contradictions might signal different segments or a misunderstood pain point.

5. Common pitfalls and mistakes:

- **Talking too much:** It's easy to slip into 'pitch mode'. Don't.
- **Asking leading questions:** 'Would you love a platform that does X?' invites courtesy bias.
- **Ignoring non-verbal cues:** A lack of interest can manifest as short, polite answers or a glance at the clock.

This structured approach keeps you from winging it. You'll find that using a repeatable framework – tied to your MVS, your outreach plan, and a prepared interview guide – eliminates guesswork and minimises courtesy bias.

Blind validation methods

Here are some different methods you can use to gather blind insights. I provide this list for completeness; however, direct interviews with potential users are the **gold standard**. Do not use other mechanisms for problem validation until you have completed at least 20 direct user interviews.

It is impossible to replace the value of seeing and hearing how your potential customers describe their problem and the pain it is causing them. The value of interviews is irreplaceable. Don't stop at 20 – that is the *minimum*.

Open-ended interviews

Schedule one-on-one calls or meetings with potential users to explore their daily frustrations. Instead of describing your solution, ask them to walk through their workflows, focusing on tasks, times of day, or processes that cause the most headaches. Tools like Otter.ai, Rev, Fireflies, Microsoft Teams, and Zoom can record and transcribe these interviews, while AI-powered sentiment analysis can highlight recurring negative (or positive) phrases, helping identify key pain points.

Contextual inquiries

Observe users in their natural environment to understand how they interact with existing processes. If your solution is for small retailers, spend time in shops, watching how owners close out the day. Look for bottlenecks, manual tasks, or moments of visible frustration. While this method is primarily observational, notes and video recordings can be processed using computer vision or object recognition AI to track repetitive tasks and inefficiencies.

Online surveys and social listening

Use short surveys on platforms like SurveyMonkey or Typeform to uncover key pain points in user workflows. Supplement this by monitoring discussions on forums such as Reddit, Quora, or Facebook Groups to see what frustrations people openly share. However, surveys alone are not enough for problem validation, as they lack depth and context – use them to support interview findings. AI tools can process text from open-ended survey responses or social media discussions, clustering common themes and frequently mentioned complaints for deeper analysis.

Diary studies

Ask a small group of potential users to keep a 'pain diary' over a few days, documenting moments of frustration or inefficiency. This method provides rich, real-world insights into recurring challenges. Digital diary tools with AI capabilities can prompt users to log their actions at set intervals or after specific triggers. Over time, AI can detect patterns, highlight recurring pain points, and surface trends that may not be immediately obvious.

Using AI in blind validation

My favourite use of AI in the startup journey is as an accelerant and aid in blind problem validation. AI can do more than transcribe conversations or run fundamental sentiment analysis. Increasingly advanced, multimodal AI systems (AI systems that have advanced voice and video functionality) can perform varied roles – from simulating interviewees for practice sessions to running Monte Carlo simulations that identify your most crucial questions. Below are several ways AI can elevate your blind validation process beyond simple automation.

Data collection and early trend-spotting

AI-based web scraping tools can aggregate real-life user complaints from public forums, social media, and review sites. They automatically filter out irrelevant chatter and spotlight the comments most relevant to your suspected problem domain.

Machine learning algorithms (for example, topic modelling) cluster user feedback by common themes or keywords. This can quickly reveal emerging patterns of frustration that you might otherwise miss by scanning comments manually.

Voice-enabled simulated interviews

AI-driven role-play offers a powerful way to refine your interview technique before engaging with real users. Multimodal AI models, such as ChatGPT with advanced voice capabilities, can act as virtual interviewees, responding in real time based on a given persona. For example, you might prompt the AI with: 'You're a mid-level manager at a large retail chain struggling with supply-chain bottlenecks.' The AI will then simulate realistic responses, mirroring the challenges and constraints such a person might face. The first time you experience this dynamic, it feels like a 'mic drop' moment for AI's potential in user research.

This practice helps build confidence before interviewing high-stakes prospects and allows you to refine your questioning approach. It highlights weak points, such as where you might unintentionally lead the interviewee or reveal your solution too soon. After the session, switching the AI to coaching mode provides immediate feedback, pointing out missed opportunities, awkward phrasing, or biased questions. This iterative process ensures you are well-prepared to conduct insightful, unbiased user interviews.

Dual-AI interview simulations

In this setup, two multimodal AIs effectively interview each other – one acting as the founder or researcher, while the other assumes the role of a target customer. Watching (or listening to) this simulated conversation in real time can be a mind-blowing experience, offering valuable insights before conducting real interviews.

By observing the exchange, you can analyse question dynamics, identifying which queries yield the most valuable responses and whether follow-ups could uncover deeper pain points. You may also spot bias or leading questions, as the 'AI interviewer' might subtly steer the conversation, helping you refine your own approach. Additionally, the AI interviewee may surface unexpected concerns or angles, broadening your perspective and ensuring a more insightful discussion when speaking with actual users.

Monte Carlo simulations for question prioritisation

Blind validation often involves a long list of potential questions, but real-world interviews are constrained by time and the risk of interviewee fatigue. Monte Carlo simulations can be repurposed to statistically determine which questions are most likely to yield valuable insights.

A Monte Carlo simulation is a statistical technique that models uncertainty by running thousands (or even millions) of randomised simulations to predict possible outcomes. Instead of relying on a single estimate, it assigns probabilities to different variables and analyses how they interact across a wide range of scenarios. This method is widely used in finance, engineering, and risk analysis to identify patterns and make data-driven decisions under uncertainty. When applied to customer interviews, it helps prioritise the most impactful questions by simulating their effectiveness in hypothetical conversations.

Monte Carlo simulations help refine interview questions by assigning probabilities to different outcomes and running large-scale simulations to identify patterns:

- **Assign weights and probabilities:** Each question is assessed based on factors such as its likelihood of revealing a critical pain point, the risk of leading the respondent, or the potential for off-topic tangents.
- **Run simulations:** AI generates hundreds or thousands of hypothetical interviews, applying realistic probabilities to how each question's answer might impact your validation process.
- **Identify high-impact 'money' questions:** Across numerous simulated scenarios, certain questions consistently produce the most valuable data. These should take priority when time is limited with a crucial interviewee.

If simulations show that 80% of the time, the question 'How often do you experience [problem] per week?' leads to concrete data about urgency, it should always be included. Meanwhile, a question about future or hypothetical scenarios may rarely provide meaningful insights. Monte Carlo analysis helps pinpoint the questions that reliably yield actionable data, ensuring that limited interview time is spent on those with the highest impact.

Advanced sentiment and emotion analysis

Once you have real interview transcripts, advanced AI can go beyond keywords, analysing not just repeated phrases but also tonal shifts, hesitations, and emotional markers. This deeper layer of understanding can reveal hidden stress points – such as a noticeable dip in positivity when discussing budget constraints or heightened anxiety around specific workflows. These subtle cues help identify pain points that users might not explicitly articulate.

By combining emotional cues with domain-specific knowledge, AI can provide contextual insights that refine your approach for future interviews. It can suggest follow-up questions targeting areas where interviewees consistently show signs of stress or uncertainty, allowing you to dig deeper into the real challenges they face.

Iterative feedback loops

After each batch of five interviews, refine your next round of interviews by feeding the transcripts into AI tools. The AI can summarise key findings, detect patterns you may have overlooked, and propose new questions or angles for the next set of conversations. This ensures that each round builds on the insights from the previous one, making your interviews more focused and effective.

This process creates continuous improvement, forming a self-correcting validation framework. The cycle of 'interview → AI analysis → refined script → next interview' helps eliminate blind spots and missed opportunities, ensuring you extract increasingly valuable insights with every new respondent.

* * *

AI is far more than a transcription tool. Used wisely, it becomes a **strategic partner** in your blind validation – one that can simulate various roles, identify high-impact questions, and guide you through massive volumes of feedback with remarkable precision. Integrating advanced voice simulation, dual-AI interviews, and Monte Carlo analysis into your validation process, you'll sharpen your interviewing craft, save precious time, and ensure you capture the clearest possible picture of your audience's actual needs.

Coping with founder stress in the Uncover stage

Let's not gloss over the emotional impact of this phase. I know why many founders hate this step. You're putting your baby – your cherished startup vision – under scrutiny. Doubt can creep in. *Am I barking up the wrong tree? Should I scrap the idea entirely?* Friends might tell you to keep pushing, investors might want faster progress, and your morale can waver.

But there's a silver lining in every negative interview if you view it as data, not a personal rejection. This data keeps you from pouring resources into a mirage. And if the pain is real, the interviews will reaffirm your direction, energising you to move forward into the next blueprint stage with greater conviction.

For some founders, hearing that their MVS doesn't care as much as they thought can be a blessing. It frees them to explore adjacent niches where the pain is more substantial or to pivot the product angle. Others may discover that while the primary pain is mild, there's a tangential problem that's far bigger – something the founder hadn't considered but the interviewee kept circling back to. I have seen many better ideas born out of the problem validation process. **Blind validation is as much about unexpected discoveries as it is about confirming your initial hypothesis.**

It's important to set personal boundaries, too. If you're planning 20 interviews in two weeks, schedule breaks. Reflect after each batch of interviews. There is no need to rush things. Write down your emotional responses and the user feedback. A founder who neglects self-care or tries to do 10 interviews a day, every day, will end up exhausted and unable to process the insights properly. In addition, this might be the time to start building your support network. Surround yourself with people who can come along for the journey and help keep things in perspective.

Transitioning to Shape

All the information you glean in Uncover feeds directly into the next DreamStream phase, **Shape**, where you'll transform these insights into low-fidelity prototypes and a rough business model. That's why it's so crucial not to skip this step. **Without user-validated pain, your prototypes are built on guesswork.** But with the raw truths discovered here, you can shape a solution that addresses something desirable, valuable, and urgent.

Some founders compare the emotional relief of Uncover to flipping a switch. Previously, they were anxious, operating on shaky assumptions. After 20 solid interviews, they either have a strong sense of *yes, these people need help right now,* or they recognise *this isn't urgent enough – time to pivot or reconsider the project entirely.* Either way, they're no longer living in doubt. That clarity, ironically, can energise you more than a string of polite compliments about your half-formed idea.

By the end of this **Uncover** phase, your notebook (or digital repository) should be full of direct quotes, stories, cost estimates, frustration metrics, or whatever shape your data takes. You'll have a deeper empathy for your potential users, and in many ways, you'll feel more integrated into their world. That sets the stage for **Shape**, where you'll begin crafting the rough architecture of a solution.

What does 'Shape' entail? It's about turning user pain into a tangible, testable concept – sketches, basic wireframes, and an initial business model. But you'll only do that with confidence if you've uncovered real insights during this phase.

So, if you're feeling restless or impatient, remember that rushing to produce a product might let you show something off sooner, but it's a complete waste of time if your customers won't use it. The time spent in unbiased interviews, hearing real complaints, and verifying the problem's urgency is your insurance policy against heartbreak in later stages.

No matter how stressful or thrilling each conversation is, remember that each person you speak with offers you a priceless gift: a peek into their daily reality. Treat that gift with respect and humility, and it will guide you towards a clearer, more validated path. Once you truly understand your customers' pain, you'll be better equipped to shape a solution that fits their needs and, crucially, motivates them to embrace and champion it.

In the next phase, you'll convert those insights into sketches and early prototypes that can be tested without massive investments of time or resources. You'll also begin outlining how your business model might work – whether it's subscription-based, transaction fees, or another revenue stream. But all of that hinges on what you uncovered here: the raw data, the genuine struggles, and the empathy forged during these unbiased interviews.

Top five Uncover tips to remember

Validating a problem effectively requires discipline, structure, and the right mindset. It's easy to become lost in assumptions or let enthusiasm steer conversations in the wrong direction. These top five **Uncover** tips will help you stay focused, extract meaningful insights, and make the most of AI-powered tools in your research process:

1. **Map the customer journey:** Don't just guess – draw a clear picture of where the pain points appear in your user's day.
2. **Use a structured interview framework:** A simple plan keeps you focused and reduces bias.
3. **Resist pitching in the interviews:** Your idea will shine later. Blind interviews are for listening, not convincing.
4. **Leverage AI wisely:** Transcription, sentiment analysis, and practice interviews can turbocharge your validation process.
5. **Stay emotionally grounded:** Negative feedback is a gift – it keeps you from wasting time and money on a phantom problem.

The DreamStream Blueprint: Uncover

The six Uncover steps in the DreamStream Blueprint – Clarify Your Assumptions, Map the Customer Journey, Design Your Interview Questions, Recruit Interview Participants, Conduct Problem Interviews, and Weigh Risks and Decide – form a structured approach to validating the problem space before committing to a solution. Let's work through each step so you can apply them to your startup idea.

1. Clarify your assumptions

What do you believe to be true about your target audience's problem?

- List your core assumptions about the problem, the customer, and the urgency of their pain.
- Identify the riskiest assumptions – the ones that, if wrong, could invalidate your idea.
- Be honest about what you don't yet know.
- Categorise assumptions into three groups: *validated, uncertain, or untested.*

Action step: Write down your top three riskiest assumptions. These will be the focus of your validation efforts.

2. Map the customer journey

Where does the pain emerge, and how does it impact daily life?

- Identify key touchpoints where customers encounter the problem.
- Map their emotional highs and lows to see when frustration peaks.
- Consider external factors that amplify the issue (time constraints, budget limits, systemic inefficiencies).
- Create a visual flowchart or timeline that outlines how the problem unfolds over time.

Action step: Draft a simple journey map showing where and when the frustration occurs in your target user's workflow.

3. Design your interview questions

How will you uncover the truth without leading the conversation?

- Frame open-ended questions that focus on past behaviour, not hypothetical future use.
- Avoid leading questions that push respondents towards your desired answer.
- Probe for depth: *what happened last time this problem occurred? How did it affect your work or decision-making?*
- Plan a mix of broad and specific questions to capture nuance.

Action step: Write 10 questions to test your assumptions while avoiding solution bias. Even better, use AI to develop these questions for you.

4. Recruit interview participants

Who will you talk to, and how will you reach them?

- Identify at least 20 people who fit your minimum viable segment (MVS).
- Categorise them into *Friendlies*, *Contenders*, *Prospects*, and *Whales* to refine your outreach approach.
- Use personal networks, LinkedIn, industry groups, and warm introductions to schedule interviews.
- Offer a clear reason for participation (such as insights, future discounts, or early access).

Action step: Create a short outreach message to invite potential interviewees.

5. Conduct problem interviews

How do you run unbiased conversations that yield real insights?

- Start by setting a neutral, exploratory tone – this is about understanding them, not pitching your idea.
- Listen more than you speak. Allow for pauses so interviewees can elaborate.
- Dig deeper into pain points by asking: *when did this last happen? How often does it occur?*
- Take detailed notes on recurring themes, emotions, and surprising insights.
- Thank participants and ask for referrals to others who might offer additional insights.

Action step: Schedule your first five interviews and refine your approach based on early responses.

6. Weigh risks and decide

Do the findings validate or challenge your assumptions?

- Review patterns – are people mentioning the same frustrations unprompted?
- Assess the urgency of the problem: is this something they actively seek solutions for?
- Identify any conflicting insights – do different subgroups experience the issue differently?
- Decide whether to move forward, pivot, or refine your understanding before proceeding.

Action step: Summarise your findings in a short problem validation report – what's confirmed, what's uncertain, and what needs further exploration.

REFLECT AND ADAPT

Once you've worked through these six steps, ask yourself:

- Were my assumptions validated, or did new insights emerge?
- How severe and frequent is the problem, based on real user feedback?
- Do I need to adjust my minimum viable segment (MVS) based on what I learned?

The Uncover phase is not about seeking confirmation but about discovering reality. By systematically working through these steps, you'll ensure your startup is solving a real, urgent problem – one that customers genuinely need a solution for. Once you've validated the problem, you'll be ready to move forward to the next phase: **Shape**.

NOTES

CHAPTER 3

Shape
turning insights into solutions

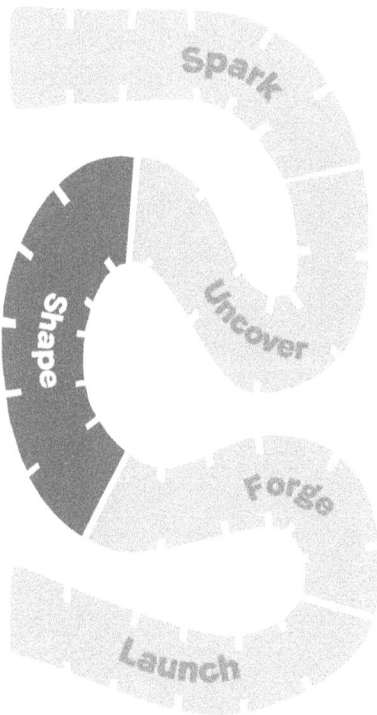

Spark

Uncover

Shape

Forge

Launch

Update the Value Proposition

Design the Solution

Sketch and Test Lo-Fi Prototype

Build Functional Prototype

Validate Prototype with Users

Persevere, Pivot or Pause

Thus is a good point to reflect. You've already come a long way since the **Spark** phase, which demanded six critical steps – from identifying your target customer to clarifying the core problem. By now, you've defined a beachhead segment, sized up the competition, examined the market opportunity, drafted your big idea, and tested your assumptions through the **Uncover** phase. It's time to turn those insights into a solution that addresses your customers' pain.

We've reached the point in our startup journey where the problem is no longer a vague hunch: thanks to your rigorous Uncover activities, you have confirmed problem insights to work with. That's huge progress! Now it's time to move into the **Shape** phase of the DreamStream Blueprint. This is where you turn all those validated pain points from the previous phase into a tangible solution: prototypes, wireframes, and user flows that demonstrate how you will address what you've uncovered.

In this chapter, we explore how to shape your solution. We'll examine how **blind problem validation** and **prototype-driven solution validation** go hand in hand, walk through vital prototyping principles, reveal how AI can supercharge your design and testing efforts, and close with a reflection on founders' wellbeing and a peek at what lies ahead in the Forge phase. Let's dive in.

Shaping your core solution

When you first confirm a genuine customer problem, the feeling is fantastic. A target segment has spoken loudly: *we have real, urgent, and valuable pain.* You've recorded quotes, frustrations, cost estimates, and everything that sets the stage for a potential product. Now comes the daunting question: *what exactly are you offering?*

Shaping that initial vision into something tangible is the heart of this phase. This is where you transform the raw insights from your customer interviews into the earliest version of your solution's 'promise' – the fundamental commitment to solving a defined problem for a specific set of people. You must be able to answer these questions before spending too much time in this phase:

- **What problem are you solving?** (Is it desirable, valuable, and urgent?)
- **Who are you solving it for?** (What is the minimum viable segment?)
- **What makes you different?** (How is your solution better than the current state?)

In the **Spark** phase, you identified a narrowly defined group with an urgent pain that is valuable to solve. **Uncover** confirmed that pain was real. Now, at the **Shape** phase, it's time to translate that evidence into a cohesive plan.

Yet simply typing out a sentence like, 'We promise to reduce scheduling chaos for independent café owners by up to 80%' doesn't mean you're done. It's less about a tagline and more about building a conceptual backbone for your prospective solution. *What specific headaches do café owners mention most often? Which of those are genuinely critical? How do you measure an 80% reduction in chaos anyway?* This isn't a one-off mental exercise; it's a conversation you're having with your customer research. Every detail that emerged in the interviews – as an example, costly no-shows, staff confusion, time wasted emailing rosters – feeds into a story you can soon illustrate, first as sketches, then as something more.

Refining your value proposition is simultaneously exhilarating and terrifying. You might be imagining a million possible features or daydreaming about market expansion. But here's the crucial discipline: you must narrow down to the core promise that resonates with your MVS's biggest frustrations. One of the big traps for early-stage founders is adding every idea that seems remotely interesting out of fear of missing an opportunity. Doing that can yield a confused solution that pleases no one.

Embrace the clarity that focusing on a single, unifying promise can offer. Lay a strong foundation by addressing the top three to five pain points your customer has emphasised in the Uncover phase. Trying to solve 10 different problems from day one dilutes your impact.

Prototype-driven solution validation

Blind problem validation and **prototype-driven solution validation** are two sides of the same coin. When conducting blind problem validation, the objective is to identify a real, urgent problem without prematurely revealing your proposed solution. This approach prevents bias and ensures you capture raw, unvarnished accounts of a customer's frustration. By contrast, prototype-driven solution validation flips the equation: now you want to show something tangible, inviting your prospective customer to poke around, click buttons, and experience your idea firsthand.

For many founders, the shift from 'hidden solution' to 'visible prototype' represents a pivotal moment. During blind validation, you've likely unearthed user pains, broad requirements, and emotional triggers. Now, your job is to convert those insights into a concrete prototype and iterate that prototype until it resonates with real users. This chapter explores why prototypes are so powerful, how to manage their fidelity (from paper sketches to near-finished digital replicas), and why founders should view prototyping as a core competency, not an afterthought or outsourcing task.

Why reveal your solution now?

It may seem contradictory at first – why hide your solution in one step only to reveal it in the next? In truth, these processes serve complementary functions:

- **Blind problem validation:** This confirms that the pain is real, pressing, and worth solving.
- **Prototype-driven validation:** This confirms that your approach (your user flow, features, or design approach) aligns with how people want their problem solved.

Most successful founders alternate between these two mindsets. They begin with blind problem validation to ensure they're not solving an imaginary or trivial issue. Once convinced that the problem is worth tackling, they pivot towards prototyping. Every iteration is tested in the field, capturing hands-on user feedback.

Imagine you have a friend who describes a beautiful painting. They tell you about the colours, the composition, the mood. It sounds great – but until you see it, you'll never truly grasp its impact. The same applies to product ideas. *Telling* someone about your concept can lead to misunderstandings or surface-level feedback, whereas *showing* them triggers concrete, context-specific responses:

- **Immediate emotional response:** Humans are visual and tactile beings. Seeing a design or clicking through screens often evokes stronger emotional cues than hearing an abstract description. You learn which features delight users, and which puzzle or annoy them.

- **Bridging the imagination gap:** Prospective customers don't have to guess how your solution works; they see it. This reduces the risk of false positives ('Sure, I'd buy that!') and clarifies the difference between a 'nice-to-have' feature and a 'must-have'.
- **Interaction over explanation:** When people start doing, they reveal natural behaviour patterns that verbal Q&A might never uncover – like ignoring specific options, stumbling over instructions, or re-checking the same menu multiple times.

Blind validation confirms the user's pain. Prototype-driven validation confirms whether your proposed solution addresses that pain. Simply explaining your solution – even in detail – often falls short. When people can't see it or interact with it, they may inadvertently nod along or politely say, 'Yes, that sounds nice', without fully grasping the concept. This leads to ambiguous feedback.

By showing an early mock-up instead of building a full-blown product, you capture reliable, detailed feedback *before* funnelling a large chunk of time and money into development. This approach is especially crucial for commercial founders whose development costs can skyrocket.

Low-fidelity prototyping: your first step towards an MVP

Before we build anything complex, it's worth emphasising the power of **low-fidelity prototypes** – whether a paper sketch, a simple fake landing page, or a basic workflow diagram. The DreamStream Blueprint includes a step before building an

MVP: a stripped-down, easy-to-edit representation of your idea. This could be:

- **Paper sketches:** Pen-and-paper drawings are surprisingly effective at sparking honest conversations. They're fast to create, cheap to discard, and easy to modify.
- **Fake landing pages:** Tools like Unbounce let you quickly build a one-page 'product preview'. People can visit your link, explore a few bullet points, and sign up for more information, helping you gauge genuine interest.
- **Process flows:** Sometimes, you only need a flowchart demonstrating how the solution works. Think about the user's path from A to B – does it feel logical and smooth?

Starting with something ultra-simple ensures you're not overcommitting on development or design. These low-fidelity steps serve as a rapid feedback loop that tests core assumptions – like whether anyone cares enough to opt in on a simple landing page. If they don't, it's a sign you need to revisit your idea (or the target segment) before investing more.

At its simplest, a prototype is an early draft of your product concept – an experiment in tangible form. You don't need elaborate coding or a polished user interface; the aim is to test whether your idea resonates with real users. You uncover essential insights about user preferences, navigational flow, and potential stumbling blocks by building something they can see and touch (even if it's just pen strokes on paper). Prototypes let you course-correct early, avoiding expensive missteps down the road.

Where to start: the paper prototype

Nothing captures an idea in its most malleable form like a simple sketch. While some founders find comfort in polished

versions from the outset, the truth is that low-fidelity prototypes –
whether drawn on paper, crafted in a bare-bones design tool,
or arranged on sticky notes – are invaluable. They allow you to
visualise features in the simplest possible way, test assumptions
quickly, and pivot without guilt. There's a psychological relief,
too: a pen and a piece of paper are cheap and unthreatening,
so if you decide to crumple it up and start again, you lose
practically nothing.

For instance, let's revisit the hypothetical café scheduling app.
You might doodle a home screen that shows a daily roster with
employee photos next to a small metric for wages spent versus
revenue expected. Another sketch might depict a text-message
reminder system, so staff receive prompts two hours before their
shift. These are boxes, arrows, and labels, not art projects. The
point is to outline the flow you imagine – how does the owner
add new shifts? What happens if a staff member calls in sick?
By walking through these scenarios on paper, you see potential
friction points. Maybe your initial concept is too complicated or
too simplistic. It's better to discover that now than after you've
spent $10,000 building a prototype.

Such low-fidelity prototyping also helps keep your emotional
burden in check. The mental pressure to 'get it right' is
softened by the knowledge that these are just sketches. You're
free to experiment, free to discard. That freedom is a gift
for a founder already grappling with the personal weight of
potential success or failure. It encourages creative exploration
without the paralysing fear that you're locked into a course of
action prematurely.

It's tempting sometimes to jump straight into a high-fidelity
design tool – complete with colours, branding, and animations –
because it feels more 'real'. But reality can be harsh if you invest

heavily in visuals too early. A visually impressive wireframe might close your eyes to fundamental flaws in your user flow. You can always layer on design polish later once you know what belongs in the product.

Think of this as building the skeleton before adding muscle and skin.

Wireframes

Not all prototypes are created equal. The key difference is fidelity – which refers to how closely a prototype resembles a final product. Early on, you can keep things simple – paper sketches or static wireframes – because you're still exploring the *what* more than the *how*. If feedback indicates you're on the wrong track, you can pivot quickly and cheaply. Over time, as you gain confidence that your assumptions hold water, you gradually boost fidelity to show more polished visuals, and near-finished functionality. This is a low-risk approach. You increase the time and money you spend on your prototype as your confidence increases.

Mid-fidelity wireframes are a crucial step in early product design, allowing you to lay out key features without the distraction of visual polish. Wireframing tools like Balsamiq, Figma, and Ulzard (in wireframe mode) help create structured, grayscale layouts that define the placement of buttons, menus, and text fields. These wireframes provide a realistic layout while keeping the focus on function rather than aesthetics. Because they lack detailed styling, users are more likely to give feedback on usability rather than getting caught up in colour schemes or branding. Another advantage is faster digital edits, making it easy to iterate based on early feedback.

Clickable prototypes

For more refined testing, high-fidelity clickable prototypes offer near-complete replicas of the final product. Platforms like Ulzard, Figma, and Adobe XD allow you to build interactive flows where users can navigate screens, fill out forms, and experience transitions, creating a realistic experience that closely mimics a live product. This level of fidelity provides richer feedback, as users start reacting to visual elements, button placements, and brand feel, making design refinements more meaningful.

Beyond testing the concept, clickable prototypes reduce guesswork by exposing friction points in the user experience before development begins. Instead of relying on theoretical feedback, you receive tangible insights into how well the interface works in real-world usage. By combining mid-fidelity wireframes for early-stage validation with high-fidelity prototypes for later-stage refinement, you can systematically improve both functionality and design before committing to costly development.

Incorporating early business model validation

The DreamStream Blueprint calls for developing the majority of your business model in the Forge phase (which comes next). Yet, many founders overlook pricing and revenue streams until they're deep into building their product. That's risky. **You can validate your business model assumptions while you're still prototyping!**

Here's how:

- **Add simple pricing banners:** If you're testing a fake landing page, include a section that outlines prospective pricing tiers – silver, gold, or enterprise. Do people click or sign up differently based on the listed prices?
- **Conduct quick surveys:** When you show your wireframes, ask viewers how they'd feel about paying monthly, annually, or per transaction.
- **Early customer acquisition cost (CAC) estimates:** At this stage, you can also test small paid campaigns to gauge the cost of acquiring a lead. If the cost is alarmingly high, you might need to revise your revenue model or target segment.
- **Revenue stream brainstorm:** Some solutions might make sense as a subscription, while others could be usage-based or free with add-on services. Don't wait until the Forge phase to decide on your approach. It's much easier to tweak your idea now than after you've built a complete product that relies on a misaligned pricing strategy.

By weaving these business model checks into your early prototypes – like showing a hypothetical pricing menu, referencing a potential upsell, or highlighting your product's ROI in monetary terms – you uncover whether your customer finds your revenue assumptions acceptable.

Leveraging AI for prototype development

One of the most exciting shifts in prototype validation is the rise of **AI-driven design tools**. Once confined to tasks like generating placeholder text or suggesting colour palettes, AI can now deliver **fully interactive prototypes** based on a single written prompt. This is a game-changer for founders – especially those without coding or design backgrounds – who can rapidly move from an idea to a live, clickable mock-up. Below, we'll explore how AI elevates the prototyping process, from one-prompt wireframes to automated user testing, synthetic data generation, and beyond.

One-prompt prototyping

AI-powered prototyping tools like Uizard have revolutionised early-stage product development by allowing users to generate functional UI mock-ups with minimal effort. Simply typing a description – such as 'a mobile task manager for busy parents, featuring daily reminders and a shared calendar' – prompts the AI to create screens, buttons, and sample content in seconds. This approach removes the need for advanced design skills, making it especially useful for non-technical founders who need a tangible prototype to validate ideas and engage early users. Instead of spending weeks refining wireframes manually, AI-driven tools generate a workable UI in minutes, providing a fast and accessible starting point.

Beyond accessibility, these platforms enable rapid iteration. If initial user feedback suggests changes to the layout or new feature ideas, founders can simply refine their prompt or make direct adjustments within the tool to create a fresh version almost instantly. This ability to iterate on the fly significantly accelerates the product development cycle. Instead of the traditional slow loop of 'idea → mock-up → user feedback' that could take weeks, AI-powered prototyping compresses this process into hours or even minutes, allowing for continuous refinement.

This speed and flexibility offer a major advantage in early validation. Instead of spending time and money on static design presentations, founders can present functional, interactive prototypes that users can engage with immediately. This hands-on approach provides more reliable feedback, as people react differently to an interactive experience compared to a theoretical concept. By leveraging AI for prototyping, teams can move from vague ideas to tangible user experiences faster than ever before.

AI-generated synthetic data

Even the most polished mock-up can feel lifeless if every field is labelled 'Lorem Ipsum'. Modern AI can breathe life into prototypes by generating realistic, synthetic data, making them feel more like a functional product. Instead of blank placeholders, AI can prefill task lists, notifications, user names, and other contextual elements that mimic real-world interactions. This is especially useful for scenario testing, where AI-generated sample entries help simulate how users might engage with a busy timeline, upcoming deadlines, or a fully populated dashboard.

Beyond aesthetics, filling a prototype with realistic data also helps in spotting edge cases that might otherwise go unnoticed. When an interface is tested with varied inputs – long names, large images, or a flood of notifications – design flaws that were hidden in an empty state become obvious. This kind of stress-testing ensures that the layout remains functional and visually balanced even under real-world conditions, helping designers preemptively address usability issues.

Presenting testers with data-rich screens leads to more genuine reactions and meaningful feedback. Users are more likely to evaluate the actual experience rather than getting distracted by empty spaces and placeholders. By integrating AI-generated data early in the design process, teams can create more compelling, test-ready prototypes that feel intuitive and engaging from the outset.

AI design suggestions

Beyond wireframe generation, AI can act as a virtual design consultant, helping refine aesthetics, usability, and branding. Instead of manually experimenting with styles, tools such as Midjourney, Stable Diffusion, and GPT can suggest colours and layouts and generate style guides, colour palettes, and icon sets tailored to your product. Whether you need a calming, minimalist look for a meditation app or a bold, high-energy design for a sports platform, AI can create multiple mood boards or sample screens to guide your design choices.

AI also assists in user flow and navigation by identifying friction points and recommending standard UI patterns. Some tools can automatically highlight best practices – such as using a bottom navigation bar for mobile apps – helping reduce guesswork when arranging interface elements. This not only speeds up the design process but also ensures user interactions feel familiar and intuitive.

Maintaining brand consistency is another area where AI proves valuable. Applying a unified theme across your prototype ensures typography, logo placement, and colour usage remain cohesive, allowing you to test a well-integrated brand identity from the start. While these AI-driven suggestions are not a replacement for deep UI or UX expertise, they significantly reduce the overhead of refining design details, especially in the early stages of development.

Automated user testing simulations

AI-driven user testing is changing the game by offering a way to catch usability issues before real testers even get involved. Instead of waiting for human feedback, simulated test users can navigate your prototype, exposing friction points early in the process.

With scripted user journeys, AI can click through screens, fill out forms, and attempt different workflows, which can help to identify layout inconsistencies or missing error states. Heatmaps and analytics take this further by visually mapping which elements get the most attention, or where 'users' tend to get stuck.

The best part? Iterative refinement happens in real time. You can run multiple AI-driven tests daily, tweak your design, and instantly see if usability issues persist. While these simulations won't capture the full nuance of human emotion, they're an invaluable first pass, helping you fix mislabelled buttons, ambiguous icons, and other quick-fix problems before bringing real users in. This data-driven approach helps refine interactions before actual users experience them.

Iterating like a pro – without the overhead

Taken together, these AI capabilities enable rapid design cycles that don't rely on full-time designers or developers at every turn. Reduced bottlenecks mean you're no longer waiting days for an external agency to make minor changes: you can tweak your prototype (or refine a prompt) in real time and keep moving.

Instead of getting bogged down in UI tweaks, you can think about the product's big-picture purpose, user onboarding, and business model, which are elements that actually shape long-term success. By automating much of the design and data population process, you also free up bandwidth to focus on core strategy.

This agility can be critical for founders, particularly commercial founders who can't afford costly in-house development or large design retainers. You can test market hypotheses quickly, refine user flows, and confirm you're heading in the right direction before writing a single line of production code.

Transitioning to low-code or no-code platforms

As AI-assisted prototyping continues to advance, it is becoming more closely integrated with no-code and low-code development platforms. Imagine crafting a polished mock-up with AI and seamlessly transforming it into a functional MVP on platforms such as Bubble, Webflow, or Glide. The future may bring direct handoff features that allow a validated prototype to evolve effortlessly into a working MVP without the need for extensive redevelopment.

Although we have yet to reach the stage where a product can be generated with a single click, we're getting very close. Once you're confident in the user flow and core feature set, time-to-market can be significantly reduced. By leveraging realistic AI-developed prototypes, startups can gain a clear vision of the user interface and data structures from the outset, minimising the likelihood of mid-development pivots. This not only saves time but also helps to reduce technical debt, cutting unnecessary costs in the process.

It is evident that the synergy between AI-driven prototyping and modern app-building platforms is set to transform the speed at which startups can launch their first viable product. In the next chapter, we will take a deeper dive into no-code and low-code frameworks.

Caveats and best practices

While AI-driven prototyping is a powerful tool, it does come with a few important caveats to keep in mind. A common pitfall is the temptation to focus on high-fidelity design too early. A polished, professional-looking interface can be enticing, but if the concept itself hasn't been properly validated that level of detail is premature.

Early feedback should be centred on product viability rather than aesthetics. It's best to start with simple sketches or paper prototypes, then progress to wireframes. Just because AI allows for the rapid creation of interactive, high-fidelity designs at the push of a button doesn't mean you should bypass these fundamental steps.

Another consideration is the risk of relying too heavily on generic AI-generated templates. While these can be useful in the early stages of development, they often lack the uniqueness required in a competitive market. AI can lay a strong foundation, but you'll eventually require a designer's eye to truly stand out.

Equally important is finding the right balance between AI automation and human input. While automated testing and synthetic data can provide valuable insights, they are no substitute for real user feedback. Speaking directly with users is essential for capturing authentic emotional responses, understanding cultural nuances, and shaping brand perception in a meaningful way.

By blending AI's efficiency with authentic user validation, you'll strike the right balance between speed and depth of insight.

Supercharging your product feedback loop

Leveraging AI for prototype development isn't just about saving time – it's about supercharging your product feedback loop. You can:

- generate a clickable app with one prompt
- populate it with realistic data in seconds
- use AI-driven suggestions to refine navigation and look-and-feel
- simulate user flows to catch obvious usability errors
- iterate multiple times before booking a single interview with your 'Whales'.

These capabilities provide a big advantage for founders short on technical resources, transforming the design phase from a protracted hurdle into an efficient sprint. As AI seamlessly integrates with low-code and no-code development, the day isn't far off when your validated prototype can almost become a fully functional product.

The key is maintaining the spirit of genuine validation. However quick and impressive your AI-generated designs might be, remember to keep users at the heart of each iteration – listening to actual pain points, testing assumptions, and adjusting course based on genuine feedback. That's the essence of prototype-driven solution validation: ensuring that every new feature, layout, or journey you create aligns closely with your users' realities while minimising the time, cost, and risk so often associated with building something entirely from scratch.

How might your product vision evolve if you could create a polished prototype for every new idea and validate it with real users in hours?

By embracing AI-driven design now, you'll accelerate your prototype-driven validation and position yourself to harness the upcoming wave of low-code and no-code advancements. The barrier between concept and reality is lower than ever – and you stand to benefit from every prompt, click, and user test along the way.

Why you should prototype in-house

Many founders discover the fun side of the Shape phase. Yes, it's still laced with anxiety, but it's also creative. You're no longer just talking about intangible pains; you're conjuring an interface, imagining a user's day, and deciding how data might flow from one screen to another. If, for instance, your solution aims to reduce staff shift confusion, you might picture an owner's morning routine – opening their phone to see any overnight changes, glancing at a daily summary, feeling relief instead of dread.

Such visualisation not only makes your solution more concrete for you but will also make it more concrete for your next set of testers. The difference between describing an idea verbally – 'it's an app that helps staff scheduling' – and showing them a rough visual – 'here's how you'll drag and drop shifts' – is huge. People can react to shapes, colours, and interactions far more quickly than abstract concepts. That gives you better feedback long before you invest in a final product.

Even the simplest wireframe can anchor user conversations. Instead of rehashing the pain, you can ask: 'Does this approach solve that Monday morning scramble you mentioned? How would you use it?' If they respond with confusion – 'Where do I see my shift reminders?' – you know you need a more prominent place for alerts. These feedback loops help you refine the skeleton of your solution. When you progress to the Forge phase, you'll have a wireframe shaped by real user input, not guesswork.

I know I have you excited that AI is going to solve all of your prototyping problems; however, I want to make one thing very clear – you, the founder, should be doing the prototyping (with or without the help of AI). Understandably, a founder might think, *I'll just outsource my prototype creation – designers can do that better than me.* Don't do this.

There are compelling reasons to prototype yourself rather than outsourcing it:

- **Scratching the 'creative itch':** Founders often have imaginative ideas swirling around in their heads. Translating those visions into rough sketches or wireframes is both satisfying and clarifying. Drafting something yourself can spark new ideas or reveal flaws you never noticed while the concept was only in your mind. It will hopefully also delay your natural urge to build software. Prototyping can be an outlet to help you avoid spending money on software development too early.
- **A deeper understanding of product language:** Building even a simple mock-up teaches you the language of product design: how user flows connect, what makes a layout intuitive, how specific UI patterns solve common problems. This knowledge pays dividends when liaising with developers or designers, allowing you to communicate more precisely and avoid misunderstandings.
- **Rapid iterations without delay:** You can't quickly respond to new feedback or test spontaneous ideas if you rely on outsourced talent for every minor tweak. By prototyping

in-house, you maintain agility. You can iterate, retest, and pivot in days, not weeks.

- **Cost efficiency:** Hiring a professional user experience designer or agency can be expensive, especially if you're unsure about your market fit. Doing the rough initial prototypes yourself keeps overhead low. If user feedback is lukewarm, you can pivot without wasting valuable cash in design fees.
- **Founder ownership:** Having your hands on the prototype fosters a deeper sense of ownership. You become intimately aware of how each feature addresses a user's pain. This perspective can reshape your priorities or spark new ways to delight customers.

Batching your prototype validation (your 20 targets revisited)

Recall in chapter 2 how I recommended identifying at least 20 potential customer interviewees and dividing them into four groups ('Friendlies', 'Contenders', 'Prospects', and 'Whales'). This same approach applies beautifully to prototype validation, especially now that you're revealing your solution:

Friendlies:
- Show them your earliest, low-fidelity prototypes.
- They're less intimidating, more forgiving, and can offer quick, casual feedback.

Contenders:
- Move up to mid-fidelity wireframes once you've ironed out glaring issues from the Friendlies group.
- Expect more impartial critique – these people aren't your close contacts, so they may be blunt.

Prospects:

- By now, you might have a high-fidelity or clickable prototype.
- Prospects resemble real customers in terms of readiness to pay or adopt, so their feedback weighs heavily.

Whales:

- Put your best foot forward – likely a fully clickable, near-finished mock-up.
- High-value, influential, or large organisations need to see something polished. If they're impressed, they can become catalysts for broader market acceptance and, hopefully, customers.

By cycling through these four tiers, you can **iterate as you go**, collecting increasingly refined feedback without risking your reputation with high-stakes targets too early.

Validating your prototype

Now that you understand the importance of prototypes, the next question is: how do you systematically test them? In many ways, this step mirrors blind validation, except you reveal your solution rather than conceal it:

1. Identify the same 20 targets:
The people you interviewed during blind validation remain an excellent pool for solution validation. They already relate to the problem. Batching them into groups of five helps you iterate quickly between each round.

2. Batch interviews:

- **Round 1 (Friendlies):** Show a low- or mid-fidelity prototype. Collect quick wins and see if the concept clicks.

Iterate: Adjust based on immediate feedback. If the interface confuses even your 'Friendlies', you likely need to simplify.

- **Round 2 (Contenders):** Bring them a refined wireframe or an early clickable design. Document their reactions to the new improvements.
  Iterate: Add or remove features to update design flows.

- **Round 3 (Prospects):** These are your near-future customers, so present a more polished prototype. Listen for deal-breakers or must-have features.
  Iterate: You're now inching closer to a final blueprint.

- **Round 4 (Whales):** Show your best version. If these high-value, influential targets react positively, your prototype is likely strong enough to proceed to the product build.

3. Capture and analyse feedback:

- **Qualitative notes:** Jot down user confusion, repeated praise, or feature requests.
- **Screen recordings:** Tools like Zoom or Fireflies can record user sessions as they navigate the prototype, capturing real-time confusion or delight.
- **AI summaries:** Consider leveraging AI transcription and sentiment analysis to spot patterns across interviews.

4. Decide:

- You're likely ready to move beyond the prototype once you see consistent enthusiasm – and minimal confusion – across multiple user segments.
- Refine the prototype further if you're still encountering fundamental pushback or ambivalence.

Handling negative or conflicting feedback

Conflicting opinions will arise. One user might love a particular feature; another might find it useless. I often get asked how to reconcile these differences. Remember to:

- **Look for repeated themes:** Don't drastically change your design for every one-off complaint.
- **Stay true to the core problem:** Revisit the original pain you set out to solve. If a requested feature doesn't align with that pain, question whether it's essential.
- **Prioritise:** Not all suggestions carry equal weight; a central theme across multiple user interviews deserves more attention than the random whim of a single user.

Edge cases and unlikely scenarios

One debate that often arises is how many edge cases to accommodate in your low-fidelity designs. You'll complicate your prototype if you try to handle every bizarre scenario from the outset. For instance, in a scheduling app, do you build notifications for employees who might be abroad on holiday or dealing with multiple time zones? Probably not in your first pass, unless your target segment specifically emphasised that nuance.

Focus on the core flows that your interviews revealed. Let the weird edge cases wait until you have a stable foundation. **If you incorporate too many 'just in case' features, you risk diluting the product's primary purpose.** This principle echoes the MVS concept: serve the key pain first, ignoring all the fringe possibilities that might only appear in a fraction of your user base. The idea of shaping revolves around building something minimal but meaningful, not a Swiss Army knife.

Don't stop data-driven validation

You might gather more customer data even in this stage. Perhaps you survey your broader contact list – still not revealing your precise solution, but presenting a hypothetical scenario: 'If you had an automated scheduling interface that saved you three hours a week, would $20 monthly be fair?' The responses can help to inform how you refine your prototypes. While this doesn't replace in-depth customer interviews, it can provide a quick reality check.

Founders often undervalue the depth of intelligence they can glean from public forums or competitor analyses. If you see consistent complaints about an app in the same space, incorporate that knowledge into your designs: avoid replicating the flaws users already resent. The Shape stage is a live interplay between new ideas and grounded feedback. You're sculpting an early vision, not locking it in marble.

Measuring 'readiness' to move beyond the prototype

'How do I know it's time to develop the actual launch product?' is a question that crops up frequently in the Shape phase. There's no magic formula, but here are a few signals that you're close:

- **High enthusiasm:** Most testers say they'd use or buy the prototype if it were live.
- **Minimal confusion:** Users easily navigate the key flows.
- **Stability in feedback:** You're hearing minor tweaks or nice-to-haves rather than fundamental criticisms.

- **Evidence of ROI:** Early customers hint at budgets, or prospective enterprise clients ask about integration timelines – signalling actual commercial viability.

If these boxes are ticked, it's probably time to head into the Forge phase – where you build the actual product, finalise your business model, and ensure your technology stack can handle what you're promising.

Coping with founder stress in the Shape stage

This stage can be a rollercoaster. You're translating insights into prototypes, absorbing user feedback, juggling design decisions, and possibly managing a small team. It's exhilarating, but can also trigger stress, overwhelm, or self-doubt. So, how do you keep your sanity intact?

Spot the stressors:

- **Information overload:** You're receiving conflicting and overwhelming feedback from multiple user segments.
- **Time and budget pressure:** Deadlines loom, or funds are running low.
- **Fear of failure:** 'What if the solution doesn't resonate?' can be a nagging, ever-present worry.

Coping strategies:

- **Time-boxing:** Decide how much time (and budget) you'll spend on each prototype iteration. This will prevent perfectionism and ensure that you move steadily forward.
- **Celebrate small wins:** Did someone describe your interface as 'incredibly intuitive'? That's a win – acknowledge it. Small successes build momentum.

- **Create clear boundaries:** If you're juggling a day job or family responsibilities, be explicit about when you're working on the startup and when you're off the clock. Having clear lines helps you recharge.
- **Peer support:** Show prototypes to a small group of fellow founders. They'll empathise with the stress and might offer tips on how they navigated it themselves.
- **Remember your personal 'why':** Revisit your motivations: Why did you start this journey in the first place? That clarity can keep you grounded when stress spikes.

Watch out for burnout:

- **Monitor your mental and emotional wellbeing:** Ongoing fatigue, irritability, and reduced creativity are red flags.
- **Pace yourself and your team:** Don't push yourself (or your team) into the ground – maintaining clarity of thought is more valuable than nonstop grinding.
- **Set boundaries for work and rest:** Establish clear limits on working hours and feedback cycles to avoid burnout. Continuous hustle can lead to trouble, especially at this stage, when user feedback loops can seem never-ending.
- **Prioritise deep work:** Schedule focused, distraction-free time to tackle big challenges rather than constantly reacting to feedback.

Transitioning to Forge

This chapter underscores a fundamental truth: a well-designed prototype can save you time, money, and heartbreak – particularly if you're a commercial founder facing high development costs. By 'showing' instead of 'telling', you access richer, more actionable feedback that guides you towards a product worth building.

When you reach the end of your prototype-driven validation process, you'll have a blueprint for launch product that aligns with genuine user demands. In essence, you're building confidence and reducing guesswork, ensuring your final product addresses a problem people care about – and does so in a way that resonates with your early adopters. Treating prototyping not as a one-off task but as an integral, creative, and iterative practice sets the foundation for a startup journey built on real-world insights, not assumptions.

Once your prototypes consistently delight users, it's time to move on to Forge. There, we'll answer critical questions: what's our revenue model? Which technology best suits our product? How do we prepare for a soft launch?

Think of Shape as your final tune-up before building the actual product. You've tested user journeys, identified your must-have features, and gleaned enough feedback to know you're on a promising track. Now, you'll formalise the build process, structure your go-to-market strategy, and prime your startup for launch – without burying yourself in wasted dev cycles or directionless scaling.

In other words, the next step is to turn your validated concept into a tangible, money-making machine. Let's get forging!

Top five Shape tips to remember

Prototyping is one of the most effective ways to test ideas, validate assumptions, and refine your product before committing significant time and resources. The goal isn't to create a perfect version but to learn quickly, adapt, and ensure you're building something that truly meets user needs. By keeping the process simple, testing early, and iterating often, you can stay agile and make smarter decisions. Here are the key principles to keep in mind:

1. **Start lo-fi:** Simple paper sketches, fake landing pages, or process flows reveal flaws early, with minimal cost and effort.
2. **Validate your revenue model:** Don't wait – test your pricing or monetisation assumptions while you prototype.
3. **Prototype quickly and often:** Iterating in small cycles keeps you agile, reducing wasted resources.
4. **Own the prototyping:** By building prototypes yourself, you deepen your product understanding and maintain creative control.
5. **Aim for proof, not perfection:** Your prototype is an evolving learning tool, not a final masterpiece. Gather feedback, pivot when necessary, and stay focused on real user needs.

The DreamStream Blueprint: Shape

Now that we've explored the Shape phase in depth, it's time to put it into action. The six Shape steps in the DreamStream Blueprint – Update the Value Proposition, Design the Solution, Sketch and Test Lo-Fi Prototype, Build Functional Prototype, Validate Prototype with Users, and Persevere, Pivot or Pause – form a structured process for shaping your early product concept. Let's work through each step so you can apply them to your startup idea.

1. Update the value proposition

Does your value proposition align with real user pain?

- Use the insights from your problem validation interviews to refine your core promise.
- Ensure that your solution addresses the biggest, most urgent frustrations of your minimum viable segment (MVS).
- Keep it focused – don't try to solve too many problems at once.
- Reframe it in simple, user-centric terms: *we help [target user] solve [problem] by [solution]*.

Action step: Write your refined value proposition in a single sentence that clearly states the problem you solve and how.

2. Design the solution

How will your product deliver on its promise?

- Map out key user flows: what are the essential steps your users take to solve their problem with your product?
- Identify core features: what must be included for your solution to be viable? What can wait?
- Decide on the simplest version of your product that delivers meaningful value.

Action step: Outline the three to five core features that define your first version – what's essential and what's optional.

3. Sketch and test lo-fi prototype

Can you create a basic representation of your solution?

- Start with simple sketches, wireframes, or flow diagrams.
- Use paper prototypes, whiteboards, or digital tools like Balsamiq or Figma (in wireframe mode).
- Walk through your solution from a user's perspective – does it make sense?
- Test rough concepts with early users for quick feedback before committing to digital mock-ups.

Action step: Sketch out a rough user interface or flow for your product's core interaction and test it with three potential users.

4. Build functional prototype

What's the simplest version of your idea that users can interact with?

- Develop a mid-to-high-fidelity clickable prototype using tools like Figma, Ulzard, or Adobe XD.
- Populate it with realistic data to make it feel as lifelike as possible.
- Create interactive flows that simulate key actions (signing up, completing a task, or making a purchase).

Action step: Build a functional prototype that allows users to navigate a basic version of your product.

5. Validate prototype with users

Does the prototype resonate with real users?

Schedule feedback sessions with at least five users from your target segment.

Watch how they interact with your prototype – where do they hesitate or get confused?

Collect structured feedback: what works well? What's missing? What's frustrating?

Identify patterns in responses and adjust accordingly.

Action step: Run at least 10 structured user tests and document common feedback points for iteration.

6. Persevere, pivot, or pause

Based on user feedback, what's your next move?

- If users love it and the problem remains validated, move forward with development (*Persevere*).
- If key assumptions were disproven or friction points emerged, tweak the approach and refine (*Pivot*).
- If interest is weak and pain is unclear, consider shelving or revisiting the problem space (*Pause*).
- **Be honest with yourself – now is the best time to adjust before investing heavily in development.**

Action step: Summarise your validation findings and decide whether to move forward, adjust, or pause development.

REFLECT AND ADAPT

Once you've worked through these six steps, take a step back and evaluate:

- Did users engage with your prototype as expected?
- Was your value proposition clear and compelling to them?
- Were any unexpected objections or usability challenges uncovered?
- Do you need to refine your problem statement, feature set, or market positioning?

This phase is about shaping your product intelligently before committing to full development. By systematically testing and refining your concept, you ensure that when you do move forward, you're building something that people truly need and want. Once you've validated your prototype, you're ready to move into the next phase: **Forge**.

NOTES

CHAPTER 4

Forge
from prototype
to product

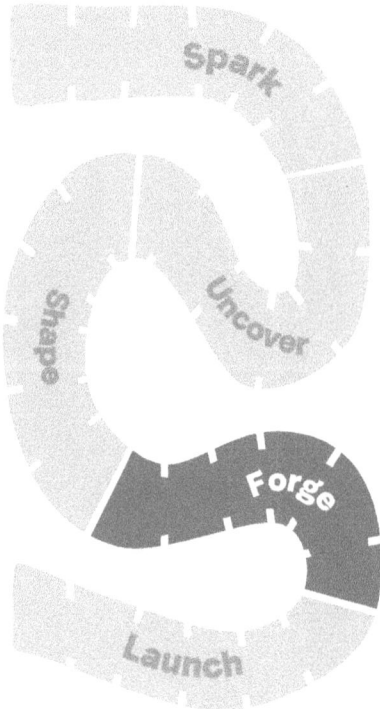

Spark

Uncover

Shape

Forge

Launch

Choose Your
Build Path

Develop the
Business Model

Validate Tech
Feasibility

Build the
Launch Version

Prep for
Soft Launch

Soft Launch
and Listen

By this stage you have laid some significant groundwork – from identifying a tight customer segment to conducting rigorous problem validation and building a prototype that your customers love. Now comes the next big leap in the DreamStream Blueprint: **Forge**. This is where you shift from theoretical designs to a living, breathing product. Sounds exciting, right? It is! But it can also be nerve-racking. Founders often find themselves asking: *what's my business model? Should I hire a development team or outsource? Will my technology choice backfire?* Don't worry – I'll tackle these questions head-on.

Let's dive in!

In this chapter, I'll explore everything from structuring your business model to finalising a launch MVP (minimum viable product), then orchestrating a soft launch that reveals any lingering issues before you go big. Along the way, we'll see how AI can cut build times, clarify user analytics, and even shape your launch strategy.

To put this phase in perspective, recall the DreamStream Blueprint steps:

- **Spark:** You uncovered a promising idea, explored early feasibility, and connected with prospective markets.
- **Uncover:** You confirmed a genuine user pain through blind validation.
- **Shape:** You translated those raw insights into prototypes, iterating your solution concept.
- **Forge:** You'll now develop a viable business model, finalise technology decisions, build your MVP, and conduct a soft launch.

- **Launch:** The stage where you go public, measure initial market reception, and adapt in real time.

This Forge phase takes you from the conceptual prototype to the functioning product. You're essentially building out the commercial mechanics (your business model) and the technical infrastructure (MVP and beyond) to ensure your solution is real and viable.

Crafting a profitable business model

Building a solution nobody pays for is a quick route to heartbreak – and possible startup death. That's why your business model is every bit as important as your product. It describes how you'll capture value, define revenue streams, understand costs, and remain sustainable once you hit the market. Think of it as the foundation that keeps your startup from toppling over.

Linking desirability, value, and urgency to your revenue model

Before you settle on how you'll make money, ask three pivotal questions:

- **Do they want it?**
- **Will they pay for it?**
- **Do they need it now?**

If you can't answer 'yes' to each of these, your business model might be built on quicksand.

You must consider:

- **Desirability:** Does your offering stir genuine excitement or solve a problem that matters deeply? Even the best pricing strategy fails if users don't want what you're selling.
- **Value:** Are customers willing to open their wallets? If you price your subscription at $20 monthly, is that a compelling exchange for the benefits you promise? You might discover that $10 is acceptable or $50 is doable if the product solves a significant pain.
- **Urgency:** Do they need it now rather than 'eventually'? Urgency can tip customers from 'maybe' to 'take my money!' Incorporate that sense of immediacy into how you bundle, price, and deliver your solution.

Each element – desirable, valuable, urgent – should be visible in your business model. You must be able to show that the product resonates with customers' priorities, that they're happy to pay, and that they can't afford to wait. The more evident these factors are in your revenue and cost assumptions, the less likely you will discover fatal gaps later.

Why your business model matters

Have you ever seen a product that looked brilliant on paper but struggled because it lacked a sustainable revenue model? It happens often – some founders assume monetisation will 'just happen'. However, a strong business model is a deliberate choice, not an afterthought. Whether you're charging subscription fees, selling data insights, or using a transactional marketplace approach, how money flows in (and out) can determine whether you're **default alive** or **default dead**:

- **Default alive:** Your recurring revenue (or trajectory) looks set to overtake your ongoing costs, allowing you to sustain operations over time – even without an injection of fresh capital.

- **Default dead:** You can't break even on revenue soon enough and must raise further investment to survive. If that investment never materialises, the runway disappears, and you run out of cash.

Needless to say, you want to be default alive! A strong business model helps you reach that point sooner by aligning your revenue streams and cost structure to move the business towards profitability rather than perpetual shortfalls.

Using the Business Model Canvas

The Business Model Canvas (introduced by Alexander Osterwalder) is a popular, straightforward framework for mapping your business model. It consists of nine building blocks arranged on a single page, each representing a pivotal element of your startup.[2]

Let's look at how each block might apply in a well-known example – **Uber** – while keeping **desirable**, **valuable**, and **urgent** (DVU) qualities at the forefront.

1. Customer segments

Definition: The group(s) of people or organisations you aim to serve. Define your entire segment but then dig into your minimum viable segment (MVS).

Uber example:

- **Riders:** People who need a quick, convenient way to get from A to B.

---

2   Other good ways of articulating your business model exist, such as Ash Maurya's The Lean Canvas. Whichever you choose, such a process is a powerful way to ensure you're covering every corner of your business strategy.

- **Drivers:** Individuals looking to earn money by offering rides.
- **DVU lens:** Do these segments genuinely want what you offer? Do they see enough value to pay for it? Is their need urgent?

2. Value propositions

Definition: The distinct benefits or advantages your product or service provides each customer segment. Also, be aware that you may have more than one value proposition. If you have a two-sided marketplace – like Uber – you need to develop distinct value propositions for each side of the market.

Uber example:

- **Riders:** A faster, more convenient alternative to taxis – with transparent pricing and real-time tracking.
- **Drivers:** A flexible way to earn income, using their vehicles and setting their hours.
- **DVU lens:** A compelling value proposition clarifies how you address the 'desirable, valuable, and urgent' problem. For Uber, convenience is highly desirable, the cost is justifiable (valuable), and the need for transport is often immediate (urgent).

3. Channels

Definition: How your value proposition reaches customers – communication, distribution, and sales paths.[3]

Uber example:

- **Mobile app:** The primary channel for riders and drivers, handling everything from booking to payment.

---

3 In the next chapter, we discuss channels in more detail, as I believe they are an often overlooked force multiplier for startup go-to-market strategies.

- **Online marketing:** Social media campaigns, referral programmes, and brand activations.
- **DVU lens:** If users want your solution urgently, your channel must be equally frictionless – like an on-demand mobile app or instant online platform.

4. Customer relationships

Definition: The interactions you establish and maintain with each segment – from personalised support to self-service. Again, we will discuss this in more detail in the next chapter – especially regarding go-to-market strategies.

Uber example:

- **Automated matching:** Riders and drivers are paired without human intervention.
- **In-app support:** Help centre, reporting issues, and rating system.
- **DVU lens:** Customers expect near-instant support if your offering is urgent. Ensure your relationship model aligns with that urgency.

5. Revenue streams

Definition: How you make money – whether through subscriptions, commissions, licensing, or another mechanism.

Uber example:

- **Commission:** Uber takes a percentage of each ride's fare.
- **Surge pricing:** Adjusts fares based on real-time supply and demand, increasing revenue when the service is most in demand.
- **DVU lens:** Align your revenue model with the intensity of the pain you're solving. If users need a quick ride (urgent!), they may tolerate surge pricing for immediate access.

6. Key resources

Definition: The most essential tangible or intangible assets that enable you to deliver on your value proposition.

Uber example:

- **Technology platform:** The app, driver algorithms, and geolocation services.
- **Brand recognition:** A known and trusted name in ride-hailing.
- **Driver network:** People willing to provide the service.
- **DVU lens:** Your solution is only valuable if it's always available, so your key resources (servers, infrastructure, staff) must be stable enough to handle demand at critical times.

7. Key activities

Definition: The main tasks or operations you must perform competently to satisfy your customer segments and deliver on your promise.

Uber example:

- **App development and maintenance:** Continuously improving the user experience and back-end systems.
- **Driver acquisition and retention:** Recruiting new drivers and keeping them engaged.
- **Regulatory compliance:** Working with local governments and adapting to local laws.
- **DVU lens:** If speed is key (urgent!), investing in rapid and reliable technology is crucial. Otherwise, your solution might fail when users need it most.

8. Key partnerships

Definition: External organisations or stakeholders that help you leverage resources, reduce risk, or expand reach.

Uber example:

- **Payment providers:** Partnerships with credit card companies to process payments quickly.
- **Mapping and navigation:** Integrations with providers like Google Maps for accurate routing.
- **Local governments and city councils:** Negotiating permits, licences, and operational guidelines.
- **DVU lens:** If your customer's need is time-sensitive, rely on partners who can deliver fast, reliable integrations – like payment gateways with minimal downtime.

9. Cost structure

Definition: All the expenses required to operate your business model, from production to marketing and overhead.

Uber example:

- **Technology costs:** Server infrastructure, app development, maintenance.
- **Marketing:** Promotions, user referral bonuses, driver incentives.
- **Legal and regulatory:** Lawyers, fees, compliance measures.
- **DVU lens:** If you're promising near-immediate solutions, you might incur higher infrastructure or marketing costs. Ensure your revenue streams cover these, or you'll risk sliding towards 'default dead'.

Why bother with a formal canvas?

A business model canvas forces you to articulate every aspect of your operation: who you serve, how you serve them, and how much it costs. You can see where your riskiest assumptions lie. For example, if your revenue stream heavily relies on in-app purchases, you must be sure your target users are willing to pay inside an app. If that's not likely, your entire plan needs revisiting.

As you complete each of the nine blocks, watch your *desirable, valuable, and urgent* criteria. Are you articulating a value proposition that satisfies a clear desire? Does your pricing structure align with the financial value users see in your solution? Is your marketing emphasising the urgency of acting now?

Leveraging the Business Model Canvas – just like Uber and countless other startups – helps you refine each piece of the puzzle. By mapping out customer segments, key activities, partnerships, and more, you'll spot potential weaknesses and validate whether your startup meets the desirable, valuable, and urgent test.

Common business model types for startups

Today, founders enjoy a smorgasbord of potential models. We will discuss this at great length in the next chapter and the nuances of pricing strategy. But for now, here is a short list. Which one best suits you?

- **SaaS (Software as a Service):** Typically involves monthly or annual subscriptions.

- **Marketplace:** Acts as an intermediary between buyers and sellers. You usually take a percentage of each transaction or charge listing fees.
- **E-commerce/direct-to-consumer:** Selling products or services directly through an online channel.
- **Freemium:** You offer a basic tier for free, then charge for premium features or capacity.
- **Data or advertising:** You build a user community or data-rich platform, then monetise insights or ad placements.
- **Hardware and software bundles:** Physical devices that include subscription services, updates, or expansions.

Your problem domain, target market, and user behaviour will heavily influence your choice. Don't guess – talk to real customers. If you're uncertain, run small pricing experiments or A/B tests with your earliest adopters to see how they respond. You'll quickly discover whether your solution is desirable, valuable, and urgent enough to command a price.

A quick process for developing your business model

Revenue models aren't just about picking a price – they're about understanding how value flows between you and your customers. The right model balances market expectations, user willingness to pay, and your long-term sustainability. Here's how to refine yours:

- **Hypothesise:** Start with a guess about how you'll make money.
- **Check market norms:** Study your competitors' approaches – are they entirely subscription-based, transactional, or something else?

- **Talk to real users:** Present your hypothetical pricing or revenue flow and gauge reactions.
- **Refine and test:** Adjust your assumptions, maybe offering a pilot or discount code.
- **Align with your costs:** Identify your most significant expenditure and ensure your revenue covers these at scale.

Throughout these steps, keep testing your 'desirable, valuable, urgent' thesis. If those pieces fall into place, your revenue model will become more robust. At the end of this process, you're not aiming for perfection. You want enough clarity to know that your product is built around a viable business model. You can always iterate as you gather real-world data.

Introducing tech feasibility testing

You wouldn't build a skyscraper without checking the ground conditions first! The same logic applies to developing a product. While many startup ideas are easy to implement, some are outside the capabilities of current technology. This doesn't require a PhD in computer science, but it does mean talking to someone who understands the technical landscape.

Before you pour time and money into building your MVP, it's wise to confirm that your chosen technology actually works at the scale and complexity you anticipate. Think of it as giving the ground a solid poke before laying the foundation.

Why tech feasibility matters

Understanding the feasibility of your technology is crucial for several reasons. First, it helps with risk mitigation – you might assume that integrating with a crucial API will be straightforward, only to discover unexpected complexities that could derail your project. Second, it ensures you have realistic estimates. If your MVP depends on advanced machine learning algorithms or real-time data streaming, the level of complexity – and the required timeline – will likely be much greater than that of a standard web application. Finally, assessing technical feasibility can provide a competitive edge. If you can overcome a technical challenge that has stumped your competitors, you may gain a long-term advantage in the market.

How to evaluate feasibility effectively

To evaluate feasibility effectively, start with expert conversations. A quick chat with a developer or technical adviser who has built similar products can reveal potential obstacles and solutions. Next, research alternatives. If your initial approach proves too complex, consider whether a simpler solution could still achieve 80% of the desired impact. Lastly, test with a prototype. If you're uncertain about performance or compatibility – especially when working with AI models that need to process large data sets at high speed – building a small proof-of-concept can help validate your approach before committing to full-scale development.

The build options: choosing the right path

Remember that prototype you carefully shaped? **Now it's time for the next big question: how do you build the product?** The answer depends on factors like budget, team expertise, and desired speed to market.

Let's explore the spectrum of possibilities.

Mechanical Turk (human-in-the-loop)

It may sound unorthodox, but sometimes, you can fake an automated experience by having humans manually do the tasks behind the scenes! For instance, if your early concept involves data classification or content moderation, you can secretly pay freelancers while your front end looks automated to the user. Many 'AI-driven' products start this way.

Pros:
- Minimal up-front coding.
- Quick to set up.
- Great for testing user demand without heavy tech investment.

Cons:
- Doesn't scale well when volume grows.
- Ethical considerations if labour is underpaid or uncredited.
- Potential for delayed responses if a human must step in each time.

No-code platforms

Tools like loveable, Webflow or Glide allow you to build functional web or mobile apps using drag-and-drop components and minimal scripting. No-code can be a dream come true for founders without technical backgrounds.

Pros:
- Rapid prototyping.
- Low development costs.
- Non-developers can manage and iterate quickly.

Cons:

- Limited customisation – especially for more complex features.
- Possible performance or security constraints.
- Vendor lock-in if you rely heavily on a single platform's ecosystem.

Low-code platforms

Low-code solutions, like Mendix or Bubble, balance convenience and customisability. They offer pre-built modules while retaining some coding flexibility.

Pros:

- Faster than building from scratch.
- More control than pure no-code.
- Suitable for internal tools or early-stage MVPs that may become more complex.

Cons:

- Still not as flexible as full-stack development.
- Licensing fees might be costly.
- Requires some coding skills – non-technical founders' learning curves can be steep.

Full-stack cross-platform

Many modern startups choose a cross-platform framework (such as React Native, Flutter, or Xamarin) for mobile and web. This allows them to share code across iOS, Android, and the web.

Pros:

- Cross-platform reach from a single codebase.
- Great community support.
- Reasonable performance for most apps.

Cons:

- Might not achieve the absolute best performance on each platform.
- More complex than no-code or low-code.
- Requires a team with coding expertise.

Full-stack native

The heavy-duty option is to go fully native (for example, Swift for iOS, Kotlin for Android, plus a separate web framework).

Pros:

- Best performance and platform-specific features.
- Rich user experience possibilities.
- Ideal for large-scale consumer apps or complex enterprise systems.

Cons:

- High costs – requires multiple codebases.
- Harder to maintain across different platforms.
- Longer development cycles.

Do you need a technical co-founder?

I know I will cop a lot of flack for even asking this question! It's one of the most debated – and sometimes divisive – topics in startup circles: *should you bring on a technical co-founder or hire technical expertise as needed?* The idea of having an in-house tech guru who 'takes care' of all software development can be tempting. But think carefully: giving away half your company for an MVP build might sound cost-effective now, yet it can be costly in the long run. And while a technical co-founder can inject invaluable insight into product strategy, it's not a panacea – every startup's needs differ.

The case for a technical co-founder

A dedicated technical partner ensures strategic alignment, offering insider knowledge on what's feasible and what poses risks. They can help shape the product roadmap with a clear understanding of technical constraints and possibilities. Additionally, having a technical co-founder contributes to long-term scalability. If your product relies on complex technology, having someone in-house who understands its evolution can prevent costly mistakes down the road. Beyond the technical benefits, a co-founder also strengthens team spirit. From day one, you are building a culture, and having a partner who is equally invested in both the vision and the technical success of the company fosters unity and shared commitment.

The case against a technical co-founder

One major drawback is equity dilution. Bringing on a co-founder typically means giving up a substantial share of your company, which could impact future decision-making and control. There is also the potential for a mismatch in goals. **Unlike a contractor, a co-founder is a long-term partner, and conflicting visions can lead to friction and slow down progress.** Moreover, even the most skilled technical co-founder has limitations. As your company grows, you will still need to hire additional developers or specialists, meaning a co-founder alone won't eliminate the need for technical recruitment.

The alternative: buying in technical capabilities

Buying in technical capabilities offers flexibility, allowing you to hire developers or agencies on a project basis and adjust your technical resources as the product evolves. It also reduces risk – if your business pivots, you won't be tied to a co-founder whose expertise is no longer relevant. Outsourcing development can also enable you to focus more on commercial activities such as market validation, user acquisition, and revenue generation rather than being deeply involved in the technical side of the product.

Balancing act: when to consider each option

If your product involves advanced algorithms or heavy infrastructure, a technical co-founder may be essential to ensure its success. Your long-term ownership vision also plays a role – consider how equity distribution will impact future fundraising and decision-making. Personal strengths should be factored in as well; if you are comfortable managing external developers and overseeing technical progress without a co-founder, outsourcing may be a viable option. Finally, practical constraints such as time and budget will influence the decision. If you require continuous development but have limited resources, the trade-off between a co-founder and external hiring becomes even more critical.

No one-size-fits-all answer

Some of the world's most successful companies thrived without a technical co-founder. Others soared because they had one from the start. **Decide based on your product's complexity, your own strengths, and how you want to structure ownership.**

If you're on the fence, try outsourcing a small project or working with a developer on a contract basis first.

The lean MVP: less is more

Let's talk about the MVP – minimum viable product. It's a misnomer because many founders build *more* than necessary. I sometimes joke that founders often interpret this as a *maximum viable product!* Resist that urge! **An MVP is about delivering just enough functionality to demonstrate your core value and capture early user feedback.** Reid Hoffman (co-founder of LinkedIn) famously said, 'If you're not embarrassed by the first version of your product, you've launched too late.'

Why MVPs become bloated

It's natural to worry that users will judge your product harshly if you don't include certain features. Or maybe your vision is so grand you want to showcase everything at once. But if you try to be all things to all people, you'll spread yourself thin and risk releasing a half-baked product that pleases no one.

A disposable mindset

Sometimes, the MVP is *disposable*. Once you understand user behaviour better, you might throw away large chunks of the initial code. This can feel painful, but it's better than maintaining an overbuilt system that confuses people.

Focus on your core promise

Ask yourself: *what is the most compelling feature that demonstrates the solution to my users' biggest pain?* Everything else can wait until you confirm your basic premise resonates.

The soft launch: where real usage meets real feedback

A soft launch – sometimes called a 'private beta' – is your chance to confirm your MVP works as intended before going full blast. It's like a dress rehearsal for your startup. You're on stage, but only a select audience is watching.

A soft launch is a controlled release to a small, handpicked group of users – often your most enthusiastic early adopters or a new group that matches your MVS. Why keep it small? Because you want to limit the blast radius if something goes wrong. If your servers crash or an essential feature breaks, you'd rather have 50 testers affected than 5000.

Here are some issues to consider for a soft launch.

Selecting beta users

Finding the right beta users is key to gathering meaningful feedback. Here's how to recruit them:

- **Revisit your 20 targets:** The same interview groups can be your initial testers.
- **Use your email list or waitlist:** If you've cultivated a mailing list or waitlist from earlier promotional efforts, invite them in waves.

- **Partner with organisations:** If your app complements an existing service, collaborate with them to recruit beta testers.

Support and infrastructure

Providing a structured support system ensures beta testers feel heard and valued. Consider these steps:

- **Set up a support channel:** This could be a Slack group or a chat feature.
- **Show testers you genuinely want their feedback:** They'll be more tolerant of early hiccups.
- **Encourage users to report issues with screenshots or short videos:** Visual context helps pinpoint the root cause faster.

Stress testing and bug-squashing

Beta users will interact with your app in ways you never anticipated. Use this to your advantage:

- **Encourage unexpected usage:** Let testers explore freely – even in ways you didn't design for.
- **Fix issues early:** Every bug found now is one you won't have to deal with on a bigger stage.

Integrating early user feedback

Not all feedback should lead to immediate changes. Keep these principles in mind:

- **Avoid feature creep:** Stick to your core promise and don't let unnecessary additions dilute your focus.
- **Prioritise meaningful updates:** Address fixes and improvements that add real value.

- **Defer non-essential requests:** File less critical suggestions for future consideration.

Advanced AI for user analytics and testing

Leveraging AI-driven tools can help you refine your product more efficiently:

- **Use analytics platforms:** Tools like Mixpanel or Heatmaps can track user behaviour and highlight drop-off points.
- **Refine based on real-world data:** Analyse actual usage patterns to make informed improvements quickly.

How AI supports Forge success

AI isn't just for prototypes. It can also supercharge everything from business model iteration to advanced developer tools and even crafting your launch strategy.

Here are some ways AI supports Forge success:

- **Business model iteration:** Tools like ChatGPT can brainstorm alternative revenue streams or simulate the impact of discount codes on user acquisition.
- **Development assistance:** Modern development suites integrate AI that suggests code snippets or identifies vulnerabilities. Partial automation can trim weeks off the MVP timeline.
- **Launch plan creation:** AI can draft launch emails, social posts, or press releases. Tweak for authenticity, but start from an AI-generated baseline.
- **AI analytics and testing:** Predictive churn modelling or user-segmentation features in analytics platforms

can highlight hidden patterns, giving you a competitive advantage when refining your product.

Coping with founder stress in the Forge stage

Building an MVP under tight deadlines, responding to user complaints, juggling investors, and dealing with self-doubt can be overwhelming. Sometimes, your mind is an echo chamber of *we'll never be ready on time* or *what if this fails?*

Recognising stress is the first step towards managing it. **If you find yourself snapping at friends over minor frustrations or struggling to get a good night's sleep, it may be a sign that you're carrying too much on your shoulders.** Many founders have a tendency to push through exhaustion, believing that sheer willpower will get them to the finish line. However, this approach is unsustainable and can lead to burnout, ultimately harming both you and your venture.

To preserve your wellbeing, adopt strategies that help keep stress in check. Taking breaks, whether it's a short walk to clear your head or an entire day off to recharge, can restore perspective and prevent mental exhaustion. Setting boundaries is just as crucial – being constantly available to answer emails and put out fires will drain your energy and leave you feeling depleted. Seeking support from fellow founders provides reassurance and valuable coping strategies, reminding you that you're not alone in facing these challenges. Additionally, celebrating small victories, like a positive comment from a beta tester, can be a powerful motivator, reinforcing the progress you're making even when the bigger picture feels overwhelming.

While urgency is often a driving force in the startup world, moving too quickly without regard for your health will be detrimental – not just to you but to your business. Time is valuable, but working at a relentless pace can lead to hasty decisions that weaken your product in the long run. By pacing yourself and finding a balance between speed and self-care, you'll be in a stronger position to make thoughtful choices and build something truly sustainable.

Transitioning to Launch

When your soft launch data shows strong user engagement (and your MVP doesn't burst into flames under modest stress), you'll finally be ready for your public debut. This is the transition to the **Launch** phase, where you'll open the gates for everyone and focus on customer acquisition at scale.

Are you ready for the spotlight?

Take a moment to reflect: *how do you want to position your product when the doors open?* That's a question we'll answer in the next chapter, where we'll delve into marketing strategies, user acquisition tactics, and how to keep iterating when the first wave of public feedback rolls in. Let's forge ahead. Your users are waiting!

But don't rush. If critical issues or user confusion remain, keep forging for longer. The bigger your official launch, the more eyes will be on you, and the less tolerance the market will have for big blunders. A well-orchestrated Forge stage will set your product up for a smoother entrance into the world.

Top five Forge tips to remember

Building a successful product isn't just about having a great idea – it's about validating, refining, and ensuring both technical and business viability before scaling up. A smart approach to prototyping helps you catch potential roadblocks early, test your core features in real-world conditions, and confirm that your business model is sustainable. By staying lean and launching strategically, you can minimise risk and maximise your chances of success. Here's how to do it right:

1. **Validate tech feasibility early:** Don't skip checking scalability and AI constraints before you commit to building.
2. **Keep testing functional prototypes:** To refine core features, use real-world pilots, usability studies, and small-scale beta tests.
3. **Mind your business model:** Make sure you understand exactly how revenue will flow, or you risk being default dead.
4. **Stay lean with your MVP:** Start with the minimal feature set that proves your core value – discard the rest for now.
5. **Soft launch before going big:** A private beta gives you room to fix showstopper issues without damaging your reputation.

The DreamStream Blueprint: Forge

Now that you've explored the fundamentals of building a business model, finalising technology choices, and preparing for launch, it's time to put it all into action. The six steps of the Forge phase will help you move from theory to execution in a structured way.

Use this section as a hands-on guide to work through each step in alignment with your own startup journey.

1. Choose your build path

The first step is deciding how you will bring your product to life. You now have several options, from no-code and low-code solutions to full-stack native development. Reflect on these key questions:

- Do you have in-house technical expertise, or do you need to outsource development?
- Is a no-code/low-code approach sufficient for your MVP, or do you require custom development?
- How will your technology choice impact your timeline and costs?

Action step: Take time to research and, if possible, prototype with simple tools to test feasibility before committing to a full build. If you're considering a technical co-founder, weigh the pros and cons carefully.

2. Develop the business model

A great product without a viable business model is a ticking time bomb. Your model should be based on desirability, value, and urgency (DVU). Work through these questions:

- Who are your target customers, and what segments will you serve?
- How will you monetise – subscription, freemium, marketplace, or transactional?

- Have you validated that your target users will pay for your product at your intended price?
- How do your costs compare to expected revenue, and are you tracking towards 'default alive' status?

Action step: Use the Business Model Canvas to document your model and identify potential weaknesses before you move forward.

3. Validate tech feasibility

Before you invest significant resources into development, confirm that your technology will work at the required scale. Here's how:

- Consult technical experts to assess risks and constraints.
- Build a proof-of-concept or small-scale prototype to test the core functionality.
- Consider alternative approaches if the initial plan proves too complex or costly.

Action step: Ensure you validate your chosen tech stack thoroughly before implementation to avoid costly setbacks if it fails to deliver as expected.

4. Build the launch version

This is where your MVP takes shape. Avoid the temptation to build too many features – focus on the minimum set required to solve the users' core problem.

- Define the absolute must-have features for launch and cut anything non-essential.

- Use agile development cycles to iterate quickly and adapt based on feedback.
- Ensure your backend infrastructure can support your expected early users without crashes.
- If using AI, confirm that its performance meets real-world user needs.

Action step: Focus on launching your MVP quickly to gather insights and adapt, rather than striving for perfection.

5. Prep for soft launch

Before opening your product to the public, conduct a soft launch with a small, controlled group. This allows you to identify issues, refine messaging, and stress-test your infrastructure.

- Select a beta group that closely resembles your target audience.
- Set up dedicated support channels to gather feedback efficiently.
- Monitor technical performance and fix critical bugs before scaling.
- Use analytics to assess user engagement and pain points.

Action step: Complete this step to identify and address potential issues before expanding to a broader audience, ensuring a smooth launch.

6. Soft launch and listen

Now, the real test begins. Your product is in users' hands, and their reactions will shape its future.

- Closely track key metrics such as user retention, conversion rates, and engagement.
- Identify and prioritise urgent fixes – both technical and UX-related.
- Pay attention to qualitative feedback: what are users saying? Where do they struggle?
- Resist feature creep – focus on refining what's already there before adding more.
- If adoption is slow, revisit your business model or value proposition.

Action step: Prioritise learning from your early adopters. Gather feedback and iterate to strengthen your final product before full launch.

REFLECT AND ADAPT

If you've successfully navigated the Forge phase, congratulations – you've turned an idea into a working product! But this is just the beginning. In the next phase, **Launch**, you'll take your product to a broader audience, refine your go-to-market strategy, and scale user adoption.

Are you ready to step into the spotlight? Let's launch!

NOTES

CHAPTER 5

Launch *
ready, set, go-live

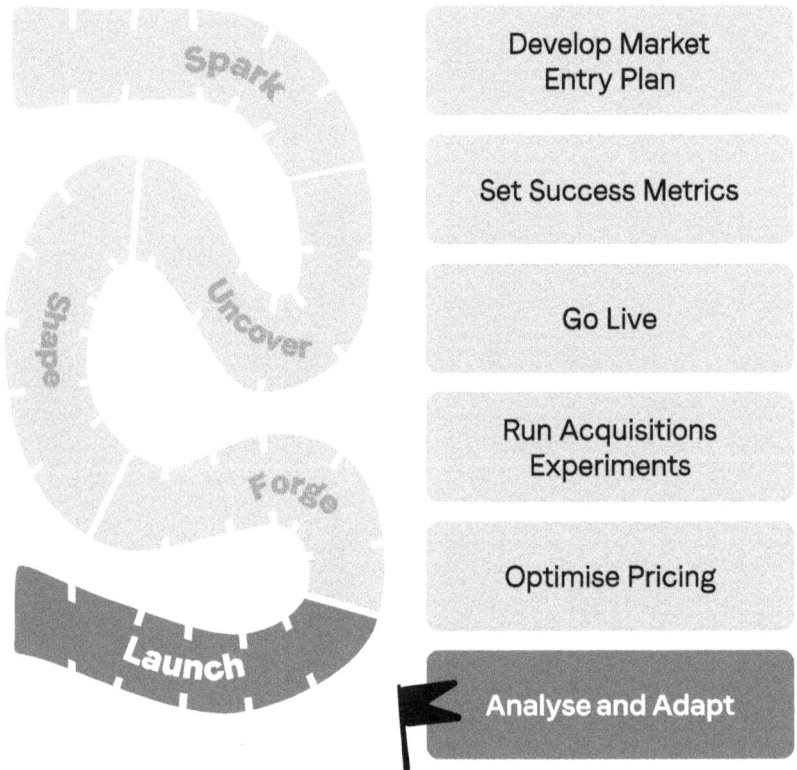

- Develop Market Entry Plan
- Set Success Metrics
- Go Live
- Run Acquisitions Experiments
- Optimise Pricing
- Analyse and Adapt

You've nailed down a real problem, crafted a prototype, and forged a functioning product. It's time to let the world see what you've built – exciting, right? Welcome to **Launch** in the DreamStream Blueprint. In this chapter, we'll look at what it means to 'go live' in a way that sets you up for immediate momentum and long-term success.

We'll explore the nuances of go-to-market (GTM) strategies, wrestle with the tension between your price point and customer acquisition costs, highlight the dreaded 'zone of death', and outline key success metrics that align with desirability, value, and urgency. We'll also address the reality that no launch is ever perfect. When you go live, you'll find unexpected challenges – technical hiccups, marketing misfires, or user confusion. But don't worry; you'll also have the chance to iterate, test new acquisition channels, play with pricing, and harness AI-driven insights to keep you on track.

Finally, we'll return to the very human side of this journey. Launch day can trigger an adrenaline rush – followed by the potential heartbreak of low traction or harsh criticism. You've poured your creativity, time, and resources into this product, so protecting your mental wellbeing as you face the public is crucial.

Developing a strong go-to-market strategy

What's the difference between a brilliant idea that gathers dust and one that captures a market? A powerful **go-to-market strategy**. This is your roadmap for attracting, converting, and retaining users when you go live.

Identifying your launch targets

Which users or customers will you focus on for your launch?
If you've followed the DreamStream Blueprint, you definitely
should have a minimum viable segment (MVS) craving a solution
to a real, urgent, and valuable pain. Think of them as your
launchpad – the group most primed to adopt your product.

Why narrow in on them first? Let's take a look:

- **High receptivity:** They already feel the pain you address.
- **Concrete feedback:** Their usage patterns will highlight what
  works and what doesn't.
- **Momentum creation:** Early adopters can become
  evangelists, spreading your product via word of mouth.

At this stage, it's tempting to widen your net too early – don't!
Going broad can dilute your messaging. Instead, zero in on the
slice of the market you validated in earlier phases and treat it like
a launchpad to larger opportunities.

Competitive market positioning

At launch, one of the biggest questions is where you'll position
yourself in the market – are you budget-friendly and streamlined,
or high-end with all the bells and whistles? There are four angles
of attack, each reflecting a unique interplay between **price**
(low or high) and **position** (budget through premium). Your
choice shapes how you'll price and message your solution and
how quickly and efficiently you can scale.

Let's take a look.

Economy (low price, budget positioning)

If you're playing in the economy space, your offering is priced
competitively to appeal to cost-conscious customers. Think of an

easy-to-adopt, no-frills experience where affordability is the top selling point. This often corresponds to a transactional or self-serve model. The risk? Razor-thin margins that leave little room for error – making customer acquisition cost (CAC) and support expenses critical to manage.

For example, a bare-bones video conferencing tool charging $4 per month focuses purely on reliable calls without advanced features like meeting transcriptions or analytics. It's cheap and functional but leaves no margin for high-touch support.

Essentials (moderate price, mid-level positioning)

The essentials angle suggests that you're still cost-effective but offer a range of core features or services customers genuinely need. You're not a luxury brand, yet you provide more than a bare-bones solution. Onboarding or usage might be moderately complex – enough to require light customer success elements. Price remains on the lower side, so streamlined sales and efficient support structures are key to staying profitable.

A good example is a mid-tier project management tool at $9 per user that covers task boards, basic reports, and integrations. It offers no flashy extras but provides enough functionality to meet most teams' day-to-day needs.

Value (moderate price, balanced positioning)

Positioned to deliver strong value for money, the value segment often hits a sweet spot for SMEs (small-to-mid-size enterprises). You're not the cheapest on the market, but you're also not pushing enterprise-level features or costs. This space often lends itself to a two-stage sales process (where lead qualification and closing are distinct) or a single sales rep who can manage the entire sales cycle. Flexibility is key – operational costs need to stay in check relative to your moderately higher price.

For instance, a business analytics product priced at around $70 per month offers in-depth dashboards, customisable metrics, and dedicated email support. It balances robust features against an accessible price point, attracting companies that want more insight without paying full enterprise fees.

Luxury (high price, premium experience)

At the high end, luxury positioning implies a premium offering. You're not just selling a product but promising exclusivity, prestige, and comprehensive support. This angle typically suits enterprise markets or high-ticket consumer segments, where customers expect extended hand-holding, robust customisation, and white-glove service. Sales cycles are longer and more resource-intensive, but the lifetime value can be substantial if you have the bandwidth and brand credibility to justify it.

A prime example is a cybersecurity platform for Fortune 500 companies charging six-figure annual contracts. It bundles 24/7 on-call assistance, bespoke integrations, and a named account manager for every client, ensuring a high level of service and security.

Gauging where you belong

Where you land on this quadrant is more than a branding exercise; it dictates how you spend your marketing dollars, the structure of your sales team, and the complexity of your onboarding. Being cheap and cheerful (economy) might attract a large customer base, but your margins must hold up. Going super-premium (luxury) might yield bigger deals but demands top-tier service and a more significant upfront investment.

Ultimately, you'll want to balance:

- **Price:** Given the market's willingness to pay, how much can you realistically charge?
- **Complexity:** Are you built for enterprise demands or quick self-serve sign-ups?
- **Customer acquisition:** Can you sustain your marketing and support costs in this position?

Choose your angle of attack with your eyes wide open. The right spot not only resonates with your minimum viable segment but also sets a sustainable foundation for growth, whether you're a scrappy economy contender, an essentials provider, a high-value champion, or a luxury experience worth every penny.

One point to note is to not confuse positioning with product complexity. Even if you choose to position towards the high end, it doesn't mean that your launch product (MVP) needs to be super feature-rich. Your positioning is more focused on your brand and pricing. Of course, you will need to add more value-adding features later – but for now you must keep your minimum viable product lightweight.

Setting the stage for exponential growth

A go-to-market strategy is your cohesive plan for attracting leads, converting them into paying customers, and retaining them over the long haul. Get it wrong, and you can sink even the most promising product. Get it right, and you set the stage for exponential growth.

Price vs customer acquisition cost: a delicate dance

Here's the tension that early-stage founders often overlook: **price** is not just a number you pluck from thin air. It directly affects how much you can spend to acquire each customer. If you're charging a $10 monthly subscription, you can't pay $1000 in ads to get a single user – unless your retention is unbelievably high, which is rare. Conversely, if you're selling an enterprise solution at $50,000 per annual contract, you can absorb a higher customer acquisition cost (CAC) and still be profitable.

Ask yourself:

- How big will your average deal be?
- How quickly can you recover the costs of acquiring a single customer?
- Is this customer likely to expand or upgrade in the future?

These questions reveal the 'headroom' in your business model. If your average deal is $500 a year, you can't realistically spend $499 to acquire that user – unless your gross margins or renewal rates are off the charts. This is why price and CAC are two sides of the same coin.

Aligning your sales approach to price and complexity

When framing your go-to-market strategy, consider two key dimensions: the **complexity of your sale** (how intricate or custom the solution is) and the **price** you can command. These factors dictate the 'headroom' you have to fund and scale your sales efforts.

Low sales complexity, low price
In this scenario, your offering is more straightforward to understand and adopt but priced lower. Because your margins

may be small, you'll likely need a *self-service* or *no-touch* sales model – think streamlined sign-up flows, automated billing, and minimal human intervention. Your cost structure collapses if you try to staff a high-touch sales team while charging bargain-basement prices.

Low sales complexity, high price

If you've created a straightforward product that also commands a premium, congratulations – you have *transactional zone* potential. You can afford more marketing spend or a smaller inside sales team to handle inbound leads, but you don't necessarily need an expensive enterprise sales force. This sweet spot leaves you enough margin to invest in acquiring customers while your product remains intuitive enough that heavy onboarding isn't required.

High sales complexity, high price

Complex solutions – where custom implementations, advanced integrations, or multi-stakeholder sign-offs are typical – tend to command higher pricing. That's good news for your margins: you have room to build a more robust, hands-on sales organisation (field reps, account executives, solution engineers). The challenge is a longer, more resource-intensive sales cycle. If executed well, this *enterprise zone* can yield large deals and substantial lifetime value.

High sales complexity, low price (the 'death zone')

Combining a complex sale with a low price is a recipe for disaster! You don't have the budget to fund the necessary high-touch engagement – yet your product requires significant custom work or support. The cost to serve such deals often outstrips any revenue you'd capture. If you spot your startup drifting here, simplify your offering to reduce sales overhead or re-examine your pricing to better align with the required support.

Choosing your strategy

If your market strength allows you to dictate price, you enjoy greater freedom in choosing a sales approach. For example, you might select a higher-touch model to drive bigger deals or keep the offering simple enough that word-of-mouth and self-service can do the heavy lifting.

But if your market sets a hard price ceiling – due to entrenched competitors or cost-sensitive users – you'll need to adapt your sales strategy. Match your approach (self-service vs enterprise) to the realities of how much profit you can generate. Otherwise, you risk investing heavily in a sales structure your revenue won't sustain, ending up in the dreaded death zone.

Sales models come in many flavours:

- **Product-led growth (PLG):** The product does most of the work acquiring users. Think 'try it free', and users naturally convert over time. Great for low-complexity, lower-priced offerings.
- **One-stage sales:** A single rep or founder handles the entire sales cycle, which is suitable for moderate complexity and mid-range pricing.
- **Two-stage sales:** Split into specialised roles (Sales Development Reps, SDRs for lead qualification, Account Executives for closing). Typically used when deals are larger, or cycles are longer.
- **Field sales or named account:** You're pounding the pavement and physically meeting customers. This is high-touch, often for enterprise deals.

Price, annual contract value (ACV), and complexity shape which of these models you can afford:

- **Lower ACV:** Less budget for direct human involvement, so PLG or self-serve might be your only path.
- **Mid ACV:** You can afford some human touch, like a single sales rep or a small team.
- **High ACV:** Field sales, multi-stage processes, personalised demos, or enterprise negotiations become feasible.

Ultimately, price and sales complexity aren't separate considerations – they're deeply intertwined. By mapping these two dimensions, you'll quickly see how much 'cost/price headroom' you have to fund marketing, onboarding, and ongoing support. Structure your go-to-market accordingly, and you'll avoid the pitfalls of underfunded sales in a high-complexity environment – or the overbuilding of a salesforce where no budget exists to sustain it.

Channels and partnerships: a secret launch weapon

Many early-stage founders default to direct sales or self-serve models, ignoring a potential superpower: **channels and partnerships**. Partnerships allow you to tap into someone else's distribution, credibility, and customer base. Imagine you've developed a scheduling tool for busy café owners – partner with a popular coffee bean supplier or a barista training organisation. They already talk to café owners every day! You'll gain:

- **Leverage:** You avoid having to build an entire sales infrastructure from scratch.
- **Credibility:** A trusted partner can give you instant legitimacy in front of potential buyers.

- **Speed:** Scale faster without hiring dozens of expensive sales reps.

But remember, channel partnerships come with trade-offs. You might share revenue or lose direct control over how the product is marketed. Still, if done wisely, partnerships can radically accelerate your launch trajectory.

Setting launch success metrics

Success is more than 'we launched, and a few people signed up'. Let's tie your metrics back to the original idea of a *desirable, valuable, and urgent* product. Are you genuinely addressing the user's need right now? Metrics should reflect how well you deliver on those promises.

Pirate Metrics (AARRR)

You've likely heard of Dave McClure's 'Pirate Metrics'. If you haven't, they are five key metrics that every startup should track to determine whether it is making progress. (Can you guess why they are called 'Pirate Metrics'? *Aarrr!*)

1. **Acquisition:** How do customers find you?
2. **Activation:** Do they have a 'wow' moment once they use your product?
3. **Retention:** Are they sticking around over time?
4. **Referral:** Are they spreading the word to others?
5. **Revenue:** Are they paying, and how much?

For instance, if people sign up (Acquisition) but never return (Retention), maybe your product isn't urgent or valuable. Or if you're acquiring users but nobody upgrades to a paid plan

(Revenue), your value proposition might not be strong enough – or your free tier might be too generous.

Your aim is to see each Pirate Metric align with some aspect of *desirability, value or urgency*:

Desirability:

- **Activation:** Are people engaging quickly and feeling an immediate pull to keep using the product?
- **Referral:** Desirable products often spark organic buzz.

Value:

- **Acquisition:** If users see real value, they'll come.
- **Revenue:** Are existing users opting for higher tiers or buying add-ons?

Urgency:

- **Activation:** If your product solves an urgent need, users should jump in quickly post-sign-up.
- **Retention:** Customers typically stick around in urgent-use cases unless the product fails to deliver or a competitor beats you on a critical feature.

Tracking these metrics ensures you're not just hitting vanity numbers (sign-ups) but truly meeting urgent needs in a way that people find valuable. If any link in the chain is weak, it's an invitation to iterate.

Winning the big day

Now to the big day! You're ready to take your product from private beta or quiet pilot to an official 'we're live' announcement. This moment can be thrilling but also nerve-racking. So, how do you pull off a successful launch?

Marketing and PR

When it comes to getting your product noticed, a well-executed launch isn't just about flipping the switch and hoping for the best. You need a mix of sharp messaging, strategic outreach, and engaging touchpoints to make an impact. Here are a few key tactics to set yourself up for success:

- **Clear messaging:** Double-check that your homepage, product pages, and social profiles articulate what problem you solve – and for whom. You don't want prospective customers scratching their heads.
- **Press releases and story angles:** If your product has a unique angle – like addressing an overlooked need or partnering with a known brand – consider a targeted press push. Don't shotgun-blast every journalist on the planet; pick those who cover your sector.
- **Launch events or webinars:** If you want to create a sense of occasion, host a live demo or Q&A. This way, you can showcase the core features and field real-time questions. It's a fantastic way to connect with potential users.

Support and stability

Nothing kills launch buzz faster than a meltdown on day one. Prepare and test your infrastructure thoroughly:

- **Server capacity:** Is your hosting robust enough to handle a surge of sign-ups?
- **Monitoring:** Set up alerts. If something goes wrong, you'll know within minutes, not hours.
- **Support channels:** Even a simple email or Slack channel for urgent issues can reassure early adopters that you care.

Collecting feedback from day one

Prompt your new users with a friendly message: 'Let us know what you think!' This can be an automated email after sign-up or a quick in-app survey. Keep it short:

- What did you expect but didn't see?
- Would you recommend this product to a friend or colleague?
- Which feature do you value most?

These immediate data points are gold. Don't let them slip through the cracks. Triage them, fix glaring issues, and note feature requests. This is your real-world stress test.

Post-launch iteration in real time

Post-launch, the worst mistake is to assume your initial marketing or sales approach is final. In reality, it's just the beginning of a new cycle of experiments. Here are some issues to consider after your launch.

A/B testing and different channels

Testing different messaging approaches can have a significant impact on performance. Experimenting with various headlines or calls-to-action on a landing page can reveal substantial differences in engagement, as one version might significantly outperform another. In addition to refining messaging, it's crucial to explore different advertising channels. For instance, if the primary focus has been on LinkedIn ads, it may be worthwhile testing alternatives such as Google Ads or a niche industry newsletter. Carefully tracking results can help determine which channel leads to a higher activation rate.

Another key area to examine is price sensitivity. If there is any suspicion that a product or service is priced either too high or too low, running small, controlled price tests can provide valuable insights. **However, in cases where the user base is relatively small, these tests should be handled with care to maintain ethical standards.** Customers are likely to notice if they see inconsistent or contradictory pricing, which could undermine trust. By thoughtfully conducting these experiments, businesses can optimise their messaging, channels, and pricing strategies for better overall results.

Small bets and rapid iteration

Think of your GTM strategy as a series of 'small bets'. Try new messaging angles or channel tactics in contained ways. See which resonates, then double down. Rather than risking it all on a single grand campaign, you learn by doing small, calculated experiments.

AI-driven analytics

AI can be a powerful tool for detecting patterns in user behaviour that a busy founder might otherwise overlook. One of the key areas where AI can provide insights is in identifying points of friction within the user journey. For example, automated tools can highlight where users tend to drop off in the funnel, revealing whether a lengthy sign-up process or a confusing onboarding tutorial might be discouraging potential customers.

Beyond funnel optimisation, AI can also predict user churn before it happens. By analysing behavioural patterns, predictive models can identify users who are likely to cancel their subscription or disengage. With this information, businesses can take proactive steps, such as reaching out with personalised offers or improving the user experience to increase retention. Additionally, AI can help optimise customer acquisition strategies by identifying new marketing channels based on user data and lookalike audiences, potentially uncovering untapped sources of growth.

This iterative approach often leads to meaningful, incremental improvements. A small boost in conversion rates – from 5% to 7% – or a reduction in cost per acquisition from $20 to $10 may seem modest at first, but over time, these gains compound. As a result, businesses can extend their financial runway, improve profitability, and accelerate overall growth.

Optimising your pricing

Launching is also an ideal time to refine your pricing. You've done the modelling, run pilots, and gathered user feedback – now you're getting live signals from real customers (including those who say 'no thanks'). It's time to put all this information to good use.

Why early pricing might not matter all that much

When you first launch, pricing often takes a back seat to something more fundamental: whether you're truly solving a problem that's desirable, valuable, and urgent for a clearly defined segment. If that core alignment exists, your early adopters will pay just about anything reasonable – because the need is strong enough to overshadow moderate differences in cost.

When price is (probably) not the issue

Price is rarely the issue if sales are sluggish right after launch. The real culprit tends to be a mismatch between the product and the customer – or a weak value proposition that doesn't resonate with your defined minimum viable segment (MVS).

Examine your product and target customer to see if you have made any of these mistakes:

- **Poor targeting:** If you're pitching the right solution to the wrong people, the best price in the world won't matter. Without a tight focus on your MVS, your message falls flat – and no amount of price tinkering will fix it.
- **Weak value proposition:** If your product doesn't solve a pressing, urgent need, lowering the price won't magically make it relevant. People only pay for a solution that addresses a real pain, right now.
- **Insufficient urgency:** Sometimes customers grasp the value of your product but just don't feel pressured to act. No pricing tactic can force people to buy if there's no immediate trigger to adopt.

Pricing gains importance as you scale

None of this means price is irrelevant forever. Once you move beyond a small, laser-focused segment and aim for broader adoption – or start fielding interest from bigger clients – the specifics of your pricing strategy become a bigger deal. At that stage, you'll need to refine how you charge, monitor margins carefully, and adapt your tiers or models as you uncover new use cases.

But in the earliest days, if you've nailed a truly high-pain, high-demand problem for a specific group, *price alone* won't make or break your success. Focus first on building a product that resonates powerfully with your MVS. Nail desirability, value, and urgency – and then worry about fine-tuning your pricing structure down the road.

Putting it all together

When shaping your pricing approach, it's easy to get lost in the details – penetration versus skimming, free trial versus freemium, usage-based versus flat rate, discounting or bundling – and wonder how it all fits together. In reality, pricing success hinges on just a few building blocks:

- **Pricing strategy:** This is your overarching philosophy or framework – whether you'll aim for quick market entry with a low price (penetration) or set your price according to the genuine value you deliver (value-based). Think of this as the why behind your pricing.
- **Pricing type:** Next is how you structure your price – flat rate, usage-based, per user, tiered, and so forth. These are essentially the how. It's about choosing the shape your pricing will take to match your product's nature and your users' buying patterns.
- **Pricing tactics:** Finally, apply specific tactics – such as discounting, bundling, or anchoring – to nudge customers towards the plan or price point that aligns best with your goals. Tactics are the finishing touches that encourage action and drive conversions.

Many new founders overcomplicate things by trying to perfect every detail. But when you're just getting started, it's more important to:

- **Choose a simple strategy:** Decide on a broad approach – maybe you'll test a basic 'value-based' or 'penetration' framework – then refine as you learn.
- **Pick an intuitive type:** Don't stress about all the variations; find the simplest pricing model that users will understand.

- **Experiment with a few tactics:** Start with one or two easy-to-apply tactics (a short discount period or a free trial) and watch what happens.

Your goal isn't to lock in a final price on day one. Instead, you want to establish a foundation on which to build. Use the sections below to explore different strategies, types, and tactics, but remember: you can always tweak or pivot once you see how real customers react. The best pricing approach usually emerges from live feedback, not from guesswork.

Common pricing strategies

Think of pricing strategy as the overarching model you adopt. Different models cater to different business goals, market conditions, and customer expectations.

Choosing the right pricing is crucial for a product's success, as it directly impacts customer adoption, revenue growth, and long-term sustainability. Whether you aim to penetrate the market with low prices, position as a premium brand, or maximise revenue through value-based pricing, each approach comes with its own advantages and risks. Below are some of the most common pricing strategies, their ideal use cases, and key considerations to keep in mind.

Penetration (land and expand)

This strategy involves entering the market at a lower price to quickly gain adoption, with the plan to raise prices or expand features later. It's particularly effective for SaaS products that rely on user volume and offer strong upselling opportunities once users are locked in. However, companies must ensure they can sustain the initial low margins. Staying in penetration mode too long can create unrealistic expectations, making it difficult to adjust pricing later.

Captive (razor blades)

The captive pricing model, also known as the 'razor blades' strategy, offers a core product at a competitive price while charging a premium for essential add-ons or consumables. A common example is a low-cost scheduling tool that requires additional payments for advanced reporting modules. While this approach can be profitable, companies must be careful not to overuse it. If too many crucial features are placed behind a paywall, customers may feel like they are being 'nickel-and-dimed', which can lead to dissatisfaction and churn.

Prestige (position quality)

Prestige pricing sets a higher price to convey luxury or superior quality. This approach is particularly effective for products where brand perception and exclusivity matter, such as a high-end security solution for elite clients. To succeed, businesses must consistently deliver premium quality and an exceptional user experience. If the product fails to meet expectations, customers may perceive the price as unjustified, which can damage the brand's reputation.

Skimming (adjust with demand)

Skimming involves launching a product at a high price to attract early adopters who are willing to pay a premium, then gradually lowering the price to capture more price-sensitive customers. This model is commonly used for tech gadgets and advanced SaaS tools with must-have features for a niche market. However, companies should be cautious, as early adopters may feel frustrated or even betrayed if they see significant price reductions too soon after their purchase. Managing customer expectations and communicating value at each stage is key.

Cost-plus (margin)

In a cost-plus pricing model, businesses calculate the total cost of producing a product and add a desired margin to determine the final price. This method is straightforward and widely used for physical goods, though it can also apply to SaaS products with well-defined hosting and support costs. However, this approach does not consider external factors such as perceived value or competitor pricing. As a result, businesses may either overprice or underprice their offerings, potentially missing out on market opportunities.

Value-based (competitive landscape)

Value-based pricing sets the price according to the value customers derive from the product compared to available alternatives. For instance, if a product helps customers save $1,000 a month, a $200 price point might seem reasonable. This strategy requires a deep understanding of the customers' return on investment (ROI). If a company miscalculates the perceived value, it could distort its entire pricing model, leading to lost sales or underpricing that leaves money on the table.

Free trial (conversion)

The free trial model allows users to access the product at no cost for a limited time, with the goal of converting them to a paid plan once they experience its value. This is a common approach in SaaS, particularly when onboarding is designed to quickly demonstrate benefits. However, businesses must clearly communicate the transition from free to paid plans. Without an effective upgrade path, companies risk attracting freeloaders who never convert, ultimately reducing profitability.

Common pricing types

Beyond strategy, you also need to decide how to structure your price. Different structures work better depending on your product's usage patterns and complexity level.

Different models cater to different user behaviours, business goals, and market dynamics. While some pricing strategies focus on simplicity and predictability, others aim to maximise flexibility or incentivise growth. Below are some of the most common pricing models, along with their advantages and potential drawbacks.

Flat rate

A flat-rate pricing model offers one fixed price that covers all features and users, regardless of usage. This approach is valued for its simplicity, as customers appreciate knowing exactly what they'll pay without any surprises. However, it doesn't scale well if some customers consume significantly more resources than others, potentially leading to inefficiencies in pricing and profitability.

Usage-based

In a usage-based model, customers pay based on their actual consumption – whether that's per hour, per transaction, or per data usage. This approach aligns costs with value, making it attractive for users hesitant to commit to a fixed price. It also lowers the barrier to entry. However, it can make revenue less predictable, and heavy users may experience sticker shock if their usage spikes unexpectedly, leading to dissatisfaction or churn.

Tiered

The tiered pricing model offers multiple plans – such as Basic, Pro, and Enterprise – with increasing levels of features and pricing. This structure provides a clear upgrade path, allowing businesses to serve different customer segments with a single product. However, having too many tiers can overwhelm potential customers, while too few options may limit flexibility and force businesses into rigid pricing structures.

Per user

With per-user pricing, costs scale linearly based on the number of users within an account. This model is popular among B2B SaaS tools because it naturally grows with the customer's business. It also encourages expansion, leading to larger contracts over time. However, per-user pricing can sometimes discourage adoption, as businesses may hesitate to onboard more employees if they see costs stacking up with each new user.

Per active user

This pricing model is similar to per-user pricing but only charges for users who actually engage with the product. It's particularly appealing to large organisations that may have a mix of active and occasional users, as it reduces the fear of paying for unused seats. However, tracking active users adds complexity to billing, and it can make revenue forecasting more difficult.

Per feature

Per-feature pricing allows users to pay based on the specific modules or feature sets they enable. This flexible approach lets customers tailor their plan to their needs, ensuring they only pay for what they use. However, it can be challenging to communicate, and if essential features are locked behind paywalls, customers may feel the pricing is too restrictive or complicated.

Freemium

Freemium pricing offers a core version of the product for free, with advanced features available in paid tiers. This model is great for attracting a large user base, as it creates a strong top-of-funnel for customer acquisition. However, converting free users into paying customers can be challenging, requiring a well-designed product that effectively differentiates between free and premium offerings. Without clear value in the paid tiers, businesses may struggle to monetise their user base.

Common pricing tactics

Once you've chosen a strategy and type, you can apply tactics – the finishing touches that encourage users to act, upgrade, or perceive more value. When used strategically, these methods can improve revenue, encourage upsells, and create a sense of urgency or exclusivity. Below are some common pricing tactics, their benefits, and key considerations.

Discounting

Temporary price reductions, such as offering 20% off for the first year, can encourage adoption and attract hesitant buyers.

While discounting can be an effective tool, overuse can devalue your product and make customers reluctant to pay full price later. It's important to strike a balance to maintain long-term profitability.

Bundling

Bundling combines multiple features or products into a single package, making it an effective upselling strategy. Customers perceive greater value when they receive a comprehensive solution at a bundled price rather than purchasing items separately. However, to be effective, each bundle must offer a clear advantage over buying individual components, ensuring that customers see it as a beneficial deal rather than an unnecessary expense.

Trial

A trial period allows customers to experience the product for free over a set timeframe – such as seven days, 14 days, or a month – before requiring payment. Unlike a freemium model, which permanently restricts certain features to free users, a trial gives full access but only for a limited time. This approach works well if the product's value becomes clear early on, but businesses need a strong conversion strategy to transition users from trial to paid.

Constrained supply

Limiting availability – such as offering only 100 seats at a promotional price – creates urgency and drives action through fear of missing out (FOMO). However, this tactic should be used authentically. If customers sense that scarcity is artificial, it can damage trust and reduce the effectiveness of future promotions.

Anchoring

This pricing strategy presents a higher-priced option first, making mid-tier options seem more reasonable by comparison. Since customers often gravitate towards the middle choice when faced with multiple pricing tiers, anchoring helps guide them towards the most profitable plan without making them feel pressured. It's a simple yet powerful psychological tool that influences purchasing decisions without requiring actual price changes.

Charm pricing

Using prices that end in .99 or .95 can make them feel lower, even if the difference is negligible. This psychological trick has been used for decades and remains effective, particularly in consumer markets. However, in B2B or premium offerings, charm pricing can make a product feel less sophisticated, so companies should consider whether it aligns with their brand image.

Centre stage

Visually emphasising a preferred plan – by labelling it as 'Most Popular' or 'Best Value' – guides users towards a specific choice. This tactic works because people often default to what appears to be the safest or most recommended option. By positioning your ideal plan at the centre and making it stand out, you can subtly nudge customers towards the pricing tier that best aligns with your business goals.

A simple process for initial pricing

Even with all these strategies, types, and tactics, it's easy to overthink pricing in the early days. Here's a straightforward approach:

1. **Baseline value:** Start by identifying the tangible benefits your product delivers. How much time, money, or effort does it save the customer? For example, if your app helps users reclaim 10 hours per month and their hourly rate is $20, that equates to a $200 monthly value. Your pricing should reflect the impact you're providing, ensuring customers see the cost as justified.
2. **Competitor benchmarks:** If a direct competitor exists, analyse their pricing strategy. Are they offering features you aren't, or vice versa? Decide whether you'll undercut them, match their price, or position yourself as a premium alternative. Differentiation is key – if you charge more, be clear about the added value you provide.
3. **Test and observe:** Your initial pricing is a hypothesis. Monitor conversion rates, churn, and customer feedback to see how well it resonates. If too many potential customers hesitate at the price point, assess whether the issue lies in your pricing structure, your messaging, or the perceived value of your product.
4. **Refine or pivot:** Pricing rarely works perfectly on the first attempt. Be prepared to adjust based on real-world data. If you initially position yourself as a premium offering but fail to deliver on brand experience, you may need to shift towards a value-based or cost-plus pricing model. Continuous refinement ensures your pricing strategy stays competitive and sustainable.

Iterating pricing over time

If there's one rule in startup life, it's that *nothing stays the same for long* – pricing is no exception. **As you learn more about your customers and your costs, you might need to tweak or completely revamp how you charge.** Here's a simple approach:

- **Introduce premium tiers:** Perfect for power users who want advanced reporting, extra storage, or priority support. This can boost average revenue per user (ARPU) without alienating budget-conscious newcomers.
- **Expand payment options:** Monthly vs annual vs usage-based. Multiple billing cycles can widen your potential customers, but keep your internal accounting and tracking organised.
- **Run seasonal promotions:** Try a summer deal or a special year-end bundle. See if it boosts sign-ups or reactivations. If successful, consider making it part of your regular playbook.

Continuously monitor the side effects. A pricing tweak might increase monthly revenue but drive away long-term loyal customers, hurting your brand or future growth – balance short-term wins against sustainability.

If you adjust pricing, watch these indicators closely:

- **Conversion rate:** Does it go up or down?
- **Churn:** Are existing customers leaving because they feel cheated or no longer see good value?
- **Customer lifetime value (LTV):** Your new pricing might be spot-on if LTV improves. If it worsens, you might have gone too far.

- **CAC vs ARPU:** Does your cost to acquire a customer (CAC) align with your average revenue per user (ARPU)? If CAC dwarfs ARPU, you're in trouble – even if you're closing deals.

Pricing for growth and profitability

Don't let pricing become an afterthought or a random guess. Take inspiration from the strategies, types, and tactics we've covered:

- A **penetration strategy** could give you a fast start, but have a plan for raising prices or selling premium upgrades.
- A **value-based approach** ensures you anchor your price to what users gain – great for building trust.
- **Usage-based tiers** make sense if your app's cost or complexity scales with usage.
- **Discounting or bundling** can entice users – but use them strategically to avoid undermining your product's perceived worth.

Ultimately, pricing is a powerful lever you can use to influence everything from market perception to profitability. Treat it as an ongoing experiment tied to the actual results and feedback you gather from paying customers. **And remember: if your product is genuinely desirable, valuable, and urgent, people will find a way to pay if you show them why it's worth the price.**

Analyse swiftly and adapt when needed

In a perfect world, your launch hits the bullseye on day one – thousands of happy users, low churn, and stable infrastructure. In reality, you'll likely see some surprising data. Maybe a marketing channel you disregarded is driving high-conversion traffic. Perhaps half your sign-ups vanish after the free trial. **The key is to interpret these signals swiftly and adapt when needed.** Let's look at how you do this.

Measuring traction

Take another look at your Pirate Metrics:

- **Acquisition:** How do users find you?
- **Activation:** Do they have a wow moment early on?
- **Retention:** Are they sticking around after the first month?
- **Referral:** Are satisfied users telling others?
- **Revenue:** Are sign-ups moving to paid or expansions?

When to scale vs when to pivot

Scaling beyond your initial beachhead demands confidence in two areas:

- **Core product fit:** Are the majority of early customers satisfied and staying?
- **Unit economics:** Are you losing money on each new customer, or is your revenue overshadowing acquisition costs?

If both boxes are ticked – go for it! If your product is stable, your metrics are trending up, and your CAC lines up with your price, you might be ready to push for more market penetration. That could mean raising capital, hiring a sales team, or expanding partnerships.

If you're not seeing traction or you have high rates of churn, it's not failure – it's data. You might revisit the DreamStream

Blueprint to Shape or Forge more. Many legendary startups pivot multiple times before hitting their stride.

The final milestone: scale or iterate

Scaling and iterating are key milestones in your product's journey. If engagement is strong and the numbers add up, it may be time to scale. If feedback suggests otherwise, see it as an opportunity to refine and adapt. Here's how to approach both:

- **Scale:** If user engagement is solid, your product is stable, and your pricing and CAC align, you might be ready to push for more market penetration. That could mean raising capital, hiring a sales team, or expanding partnerships.
- **Iterate:** If early feedback is lukewarm or reveals deeper issues, circle back to shaping or forging. That's not failure – some of the best startups pivot repeatedly before finding their sweet spot.

Using AI in the launch phase

We've already discussed AI for analytics, but it doesn't stop there. AI can assist with everything from drafting marketing copy to predicting which users will most likely upgrade. The beauty of modern AI is that it's accessible – even for early-stage founders with limited budgets. Let's look at some ways you can use AI in this stage.

Marketing copy and press materials

You can feed a product summary or a rough pitch draft into an AI writing tool to get fresh angles or improved clarity. AI won't replace your judgement but can spark ideas for taglines, email subjects, or social media blurbs.

Customer support bots

A basic chatbot can handle first-level queries, pointing users to documentation or capturing their requests for escalation. You don't have to build a fancy system from scratch – plenty of off-the-shelf solutions integrate easily. Just be sure to maintain a personal human touch for more complex issues.

AI-driven personalisation

If you have enough user data, AI can recommend features or content that individuals will likely find relevant, boosting retention. For instance, a scheduling tool might suggest advanced shift-planning features to managers who frequently tweak schedules at the last minute.

Churn prediction models

One of the most powerful applications of AI in the post-launch phase is identifying which customers are likely to cancel – or attrit – before they actually do. Analysing factors like login frequency, feature usage, and support interaction, churn prediction models spot subtle warning signs that even an attentive human might miss. For instance, an early drop in session duration or a lack of engagement with a newly released feature could signal waning interest. Once the model flags a customer as high-risk, you can proactively reach out with tailored offers, schedule a quick check-in call, or provide targeted training resources.

Launch is just the beginning

It's easy to see launch day as the finish line. In truth, it's the start of a longer marathon. Keep an open mind, maintain curiosity, and adapt quickly. Everything you've learned – about desirability, value, urgency, and iterative product development – matters even more once real users show up.

Take a moment to ask yourself: *what's the next big leap?* Maybe it's forging a partnership that turbocharges distribution, doubling down on AI-driven insights, or refining your unique selling proposition. Stay flexible, stay observant, and never forget: your greatest strength is your willingness to test, learn, and pivot.

You've launched. Now it's time to build on that momentum, refine your go-to-market strategy, keep your pricing tuned to actual user value, and focus on retention. Enjoy the rush, learn from every experiment, and push forward as you continue evolving the startup you've worked so hard to bring to life.

Coping with founder stress in the Launch stage

Let's not forget the emotional ride. Launch day can feel like Christmas morning – followed by the realisation that not everyone's as thrilled about your product as you'd hoped. Or maybe you get a solid response, and the sudden influx overwhelms your servers. It's easy to feel whiplash.

After weeks (or months) of late nights, it's normal to feel a 'comedown', even if the launch goes well. Or maybe traction isn't as explosive as you hoped, or a wave of technical issues emerges. Don't let disappointment overshadow real progress:

- **Accept imperfection:** Something will go sideways no matter how well you plan. It's okay.
- **Lean on a support network:** Whether mentors or founder peers, share your worries and glean their insights.
- **Celebrate small wins:** If 10 people sign up on day one, that's 10 more than zero. Acknowledge each step forward.

Post-launch, keep a stable schedule, find moments to recharge, and watch your mental health as closely as your Pirate Metrics. A balanced founder makes clearer decisions, especially in chaos.

Reaching the launch phase is a massive milestone. You've proved a real need, built a product to satisfy it, and mustered the courage to put it in front of real users. **Whether you see roaring success, modest traction, or face a harsh reality check – be proud that you made it this far.** Most do not.

Yet, the startup journey never truly ends. There will always be fresh challenges and bigger dreams. Nurture your mental health, celebrate progress, and remind yourself that each small win is a step forward.

Top five Launch tips to remember

A successful product launch requires more than just a great idea – it demands strategic planning, adaptability, and resilience. From aligning your go-to-market strategy to fine-tuning pricing and leveraging AI-driven insights, every decision plays a role in shaping your product's trajectory. At the same time, keeping an eye on sustainability – both financial and personal – is crucial.

Here's how to navigate the launch phase effectively:

1. **Develop a unified go-to-market plan:** Ensure every aspect of your launch – from your messaging and channel selection to your team's execution – is meticulously aligned. A cohesive go-to-market strategy reinforces your product's unique value and sets the stage for a smooth, impactful market entry.
2. **Experiment with pricing:** Try A/B testing, freemium models, and selective discounts or offers to find the sweet spot that resonates with your users.
3. **Watch out for the death zone:** If your product is complex but cheap, or your CAC dwarfs your price point, consider simplifying your product or raising prices.
4. **Use AI for insights:** Leverage AI for user analytics, churn prediction, and marketing copy – but keep human judgement in the driver's seat.
5. **Protect your mental health:** Launch is stressful! Celebrate small wins, accept imperfection, and stay grounded as you face real-world scrutiny.

The DreamStream Blueprint: Launch

Now that you've absorbed the strategies and insights from this chapter, it's time to put them into action. The six steps outlined in the image serve as a practical roadmap for executing your launch effectively. Let's break them down and connect each step to what we've covered in this chapter.

1. Develop market entry plan

Your **go-to-market (GTM)** strategy is the backbone of your market entry. At this stage, you should:

- Choose a competitive positioning strategy (economy, essentials, value, or luxury) that aligns with your offering and market expectations.
- Select the best sales model for your pricing and complexity (self-service, product-led growth, inside sales, or enterprise sales).
- Identify partnership opportunities to leverage existing distribution channels and credibility.

Action step: Refine your minimum viable segment (MVS), choose a competitive positioning strategy, and select the best sales model to align with your pricing and complexity.

2. Set success metrics

Your launch isn't just about going live – it's about measuring and adapting based on real user engagement.

The key success metrics should align with the **Pirate Metrics**:

- **Acquisition:** Where are users coming from?
- **Activation:** Are they engaging quickly and experiencing value?
- **Retention:** Are they sticking around beyond the first use?
- **Referral:** Are happy users recommending your product?

- **Revenue:** Are customers converting to paid users or expanding their engagement?

Action step: Establish clear, measurable success metrics using the Pirate Metrics.

3. Go live

The moment you've been working towards! To ensure a smooth launch:

- Double-check your infrastructure stability – prevent crashes and downtime.
- Ensure clear, compelling messaging across all customer touchpoints (website, social media, app store listings, email campaigns).
- Use AI-driven tools to automate support responses and guide users through onboarding.
- Prepare a plan for handling technical issues and user feedback in real time.

Action step: Have a plan in place for real-time technical issue resolution and user feedback handling.

4. Run acquisition experiments

A successful launch doesn't stop at going live. It requires continuous **testing and iteration** to find the most effective acquisition strategies. Consider:

- A/B testing different marketing messages to determine what resonates most with your audience.
- Experimenting with different ad channels (such as LinkedIn vs Google Ads vs influencer marketing).

- Running small pricing experiments to gauge elasticity without alienating early adopters.
- Using AI-driven insights to analyse user behaviour and drop-off points, refining your onboarding or marketing funnel accordingly.

Action step: Continuously test and iterate on acquisition strategies by A/B testing messaging, experimenting with different ad channels, and refining pricing approaches. Use AI-driven insights to identify drop-off points and improve onboarding.

5. Optimise pricing

Your pricing model is not set in stone. Post-launch data will reveal whether adjustments are needed. To refine your pricing:

- Compare real user behaviour to your original pricing hypotheses.
- Identify if users are churning due to pricing resistance or lack of perceived value.
- Consider introducing premium tiers or bundling options to increase revenue without losing price-sensitive users.
- Monitor your customer acquisition cost (CAC) vs lifetime value (LTV) to ensure long-term profitability.

Action step: Analyse post-launch user behaviour to assess pricing effectiveness. Identify churn causes, test premium tiers or bundles, and monitor CAC vs LTV to maintain profitability while maximising user retention.

6. Analyse and adapt

The final step is about **continuous learning and iteration**. No launch is perfect, but your ability to analyse and adapt will define your long-term success. Focus on:

- Spotting trends in engagement and churn – are certain features more popular than expected? Are users dropping off at a predictable stage?
- Scaling what works – double down on the most effective marketing channels and acquisition strategies.
- Pivoting if necessary – if initial feedback suggests a mismatch in positioning or pricing, be ready to tweak your approach.
- Maintaining founder resilience – launching is emotionally intense, so keep perspective, seek support, and celebrate small wins.

Action step: Regularly review engagement trends, double down on what works, and pivot if needed based on user feedback.

REFLECT AND ADAPT

Your launch isn't just a single event – it's an ongoing process of **refinement, iteration, and scaling**. By systematically working through these six steps, you'll be able to adapt in real-time, strengthen your market position, and set your product up for long-term success. Stay agile, listen to your customers, and remember: launch is just the beginning!

NOTES

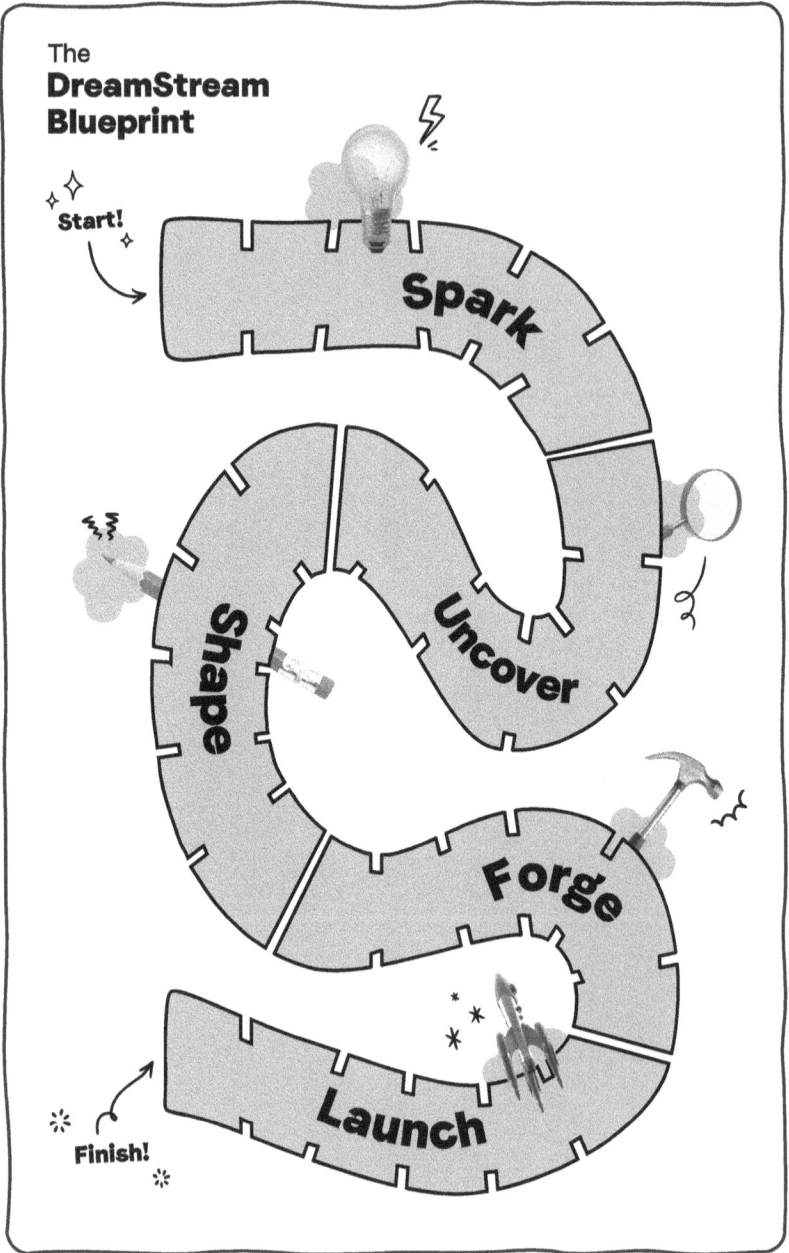

The
DreamStream Blueprint

Start!

Spark

Uncover

Shape

Forge

Launch

Finish!

Starting is easy, staying is harder

A business partner once told me that starting a business is easy; continuing beyond the honeymoon phase is where reality sets in. As I conclude this book, I find that statement rings truer than ever. In these pages, I have distilled a methodical approach: mapping out each phase of moving from a raw idea to a launched startup, validating at every turn, and harnessing new accelerators like AI. Yet everything we have explored is just the beginning. **A startup never stands still. It is either in the process of growing, adapting, and learning, or it is in the process of dying.**

Countless ideas are swirling around the world – lightbulb moments that flash in people's minds while showering, daydreaming, or ranting about products that they hate. Yet most ideas never see daylight, not because they lack merit, but because the path to turn them into functioning ventures is freaking hard! It is far easier to keep fantasies in your head than to face the emotional rigour of building something tangible, testing it with actual users, and confronting the potential heartbreak of failure. I hope this book has given you the means to narrow the chasm between raw dreams and working realities – an approach that acknowledges the vital discipline of systematic validation and the personal toll on those who attempt it.

Genuinely great founders are not just obsessed with their solutions but with learning. They devour new data, cling to fresh insights, chase user feedback, and pivot rapidly when they realise they are heading in the wrong direction. These founders do not see iteration as a chore; they see it as the lifeblood of innovation. In many ways, their product is not the app they publish or the service they sell but the process by which they keep refining, adjusting, and improving. Every day, they refine their craft, always hungering for that next insight that can turbocharge growth or stave off the constant threat of extinction. This mindset sets them apart from founders who cling stubbornly to a single approach, ignoring the evidence stacking up around them.

In the past, such relentless learning might have seemed tedious. You would do your customer interviews, pore over spreadsheets, and grit your teeth at the slow pace of coding. However, founders in the current generation have a potent advantage that was scarcely imaginable a few short years ago: artificial intelligence. AI is no longer the distant sci-fi concept it used to be. It is a hands-on ally that can help you with everything from brainstorming ideas and generating user insights to rapidly prototyping designs and performing complex analyses you do not have time to do manually. **I now consider AI as another member of my co-founding team – one that argues with me less!**

This means that the leaps of faith that once required lots of capital or a dedicated technical co-founder can now be approached in a far more streamlined, evidence-based manner.

If you are a commercial founder who used to feel locked out of high-tech development, AI can reduce your dependence on expensive dev agencies or complex coding tasks, letting you stay nimble. If you are a technical founder, AI can lift some of the heaviest programming drudgery off your plate, accelerating your progress so that you can focus on strategic product decisions. By removing tedious barriers, AI gives you back hours or days each week to invest in what truly matters: listening to users, refining your approach, and evolving your product to match actual needs.

Throughout these chapters, we have explored how to define a minimum viable segment – because starting small and focused is the key to early traction. We have emphasised blind problem validation – because hearing genuine customer pain is more reliable than listening to polite 'Yes, that's interesting' compliments. I have championed prototype-driven solution validation – because you only discover actual user responses once they can see or feel what you have created. I have repeatedly noted how AI can slot into each step, fast-tracking you beyond the bottlenecks that used to plague early-stage founders.

Yet, even if you adopt every recommendation in this book, the path remains challenging. Ideas do not magically become million-dollar ventures by following a few bullet points. As I said from the outset, this is the start of a journey, not its culmination. The next wave of user feedback might force you to remove some features you felt sure about. The next shift in economic climate might disrupt your go-to-market strategy. The next AI breakthrough might negate half of your coding or design assumptions. Building a startup is dynamic and sometimes ferociously stressful. But if you use the frameworks laid out here, you will find you are more adaptable, less likely to be caught flat-footed, and better equipped to pivot when the winds of change blow through.

I have often heard people lament that 'It's never been harder to start a venture' because so many industries are saturated, competition is fierce, and trends come and go faster than ever. But I would counter that it has also never been easier to test your assumptions quickly, never more affordable to build a working MVP, and never more feasible for non-technical founders to harness top-tier tech. And it has certainly never been a more promising time to harness AI for everything from lead scoring to advanced design generation. This duality – greater market noise, yet more effective tools for rising above it – means you can succeed if you adopt a methodical, focused approach. Attempting to replicate success stories through hustle or hype no longer cuts it.

When I spoke earlier about the reality of ideas that never get off the ground, I had in mind those side-hustle entrepreneurs who daydream for years but are terrified to truly commit to building something. I also had in mind the cautious employees who keep a brilliant concept locked away because they fear the risk is too high. The truth is that you do not have to sabotage your entire life to test an idea. You don't have to quit your day job to experiment. By focusing on the core steps – identifying a pinpoint MVS, verifying the problem, shaping low-cost prototypes, forging an MVP with targeted AI-driven support, and launching in a disciplined manner – you can dramatically lower the stakes of your gamble. You can run these steps while working a day job if you partition your time carefully. Or you can do them as a full-time founder without burning your resources too quickly. The process is not easy, but it is far more science than blind guesswork.

Science, however, does not mean devoid of passion. This approach embraces the idea that you care deeply about solving a fundamental human problem. You are not just flipping domain names or chasing the latest trend, hoping for a quick exit. You are forging a solution that might reshape how a small group of people cope with their daily frustrations – whether that is scheduling staff, managing finances, or something else entirely. That sense of mission can carry you through the inevitable nights of frustration. The moment you see a user genuinely rely on your product to solve a problem, you realise the difference between 'a nice idea' and 'a truly indispensable tool'.

You might wonder: *but how do I know if my new idea will stand out in such a cluttered market?* And the honest answer is that you do not know until you test it. The best approach is to keep your idea small but ambitious, validated by real user pain, hammered into shape by honest user feedback, accelerated by carefully chosen AI technology, and tested in actual user environments before you blow tens of thousands of dollars. If it turns out to be not hitting the mark, you can pivot or part ways with the concept with minimal regrets, having spent a fraction of the resources you might have wasted otherwise. If it hits, you double down with the confidence that your data, rather than your ego, justifies that expansion.

This generation of founders has a distinct advantage over the last precisely because AI supercharges each phase. In years past, you might have spent your first $20,000 building an MVP from scratch or hiring a data scientist for tasks that can now be automated. That difference alone can be the margin between success and failure. But do not mistake AI for a silver bullet; it requires strategic integration, not a mindless trust that technology will solve everything. AI can code a skeleton but cannot automatically deliver empathetic customer research. AI can produce marketing text, but it cannot replicate the genuine connection you forge when you engage with your potential customers. Ultimately, it is an enabler, a set of powerful tools that amplify your methodology. **The real artistry still comes from your empathy, customer interviews, willingness to pivot, and readiness to refine features until they click.**

The conclusion of this book, then, is hardly a final stop. It is an invitation to begin, to keep learning, to harness the new AI era, to run your experiments with rigour, to treat user validation as a non-negotiable, to stay mindful of your boundaries, and to remain open to the possibility that your initial idea might morph into something even more powerful once real users get their hands on it. If that sounds uncertain, it is – startups thrive on uncertainty. However, that same uncertainty holds tremendous promise for founders who can systematically test assumptions and adapt with agility.

So, I'd like to leave you with a sense of hope and a call to action: do not let your idea wither in the realm of 'someday I'll do it'. You have a method, the possibility of AI as an accelerant, and the capacity to pace your emotional investment so you do not break under pressure. To see real progress, start small, stay user-centric, refine prototypes, leverage AI as a tool rather than a crutch, and move forward one validated step at a time. Let the DreamStream Blueprint guide you, letting each phase build naturally on the last until you stand on the cusp of a workable product that can stand up in the real world.

There is no guarantee of a billion-dollar exit – nor should that be your only measure of success. Often, a well-run startup that pays your bills, solves an authentic customer need, and fosters a healthy work-life balance, is a bigger victory than chasing unicorn status. The world has enough half-finished platforms that began in a blaze of hype and died from a lack of realistic validation. Let your creation be the one that stands up, goes to market, and endures. Because while there are a million ideas out there, only a fraction will become living, breathing ventures. Among those that do, many will fail due to poor focus or over-ambition. By following a measured path, you shift the odds in your favour.

Call it science, craft, or an ever-evolving discipline – building a startup can be broken down into steps that reduce guesswork and increase the probability of success. That might be the greatest gift you can give yourself as a founder: the knowledge that you did not just fling an idea into the void and hope it worked but methodically shaped it into something that resonates deeply with an urgent problem. This book has been about removing illusions, clarifying your process, and giving you the impetus to refine your skill set.

So go forth with optimism. Let your new product gather real users, accept that you will adapt to their feedback, embrace the next wave of AI breakthroughs, and keep your eyes fixed on sustainably solving authentic problems. This book closes, but your journey is just beginning. There will be further lessons, fresh obstacles, new technology waves, and expansions you cannot currently imagine. All of that is the best part because the essence of being a founder is living in that space where tomorrow's challenges sharpen you rather than defeat you.

You have a plan, a blueprint, a sense of how to keep your wellbeing intact, and the unstoppable force of AI at your fingertips. The rest, as they say, is up to you. Go make something that matters. The world could use a few more dedicated founders who know exactly how to validate and deliver on the real needs around them. With a bit of luck and a methodical approach, you might be the one who turns a modest spark into a bright and enduring flame. Oh, and don't forget your friends when you make it.

To those who made it happen

To my family – words could never truly capture the depth of my gratitude for your unwavering support. You've cheered me on through every hare-brained pivot, tolerated endless late-night rewrites, and patiently endured caffeine-fuelled brainstorms that bordered on madness. You've been my rock, my refuge, and my loudest cheerleaders. I love you more fiercely than I can express – thank you for everything. **Peter Durie** – my oldest and dearest friend. From AAAArdvark and Thorpe suits to now just two old blokes shouting at the telly, you've always been right there beside me. Here's to becoming even grumpier old men together – I wouldn't have it any other way. **Melissa Cupples** – my best friend, stoic sister, and easily the worst responder to text messages I've ever known. You are my intellectual stimulant, my Marcus Aurelius on speed dial, and the one who constantly challenges and inspires me. Our philosophical debates are oxygen for my soul; I couldn't imagine navigating life without your wisdom, laughter, and occasional, spectacular silence. **Matt Church**, my mentor, sage, and elder – you consistently challenge and inspire me, reminding me that wisdom truly does come with experience. And of course, **Olivia Tyler** and **Sonja Busse** – the Clams – your love, support, and endless laughter have repeatedly prevented me from hiding under the house curled up like a cat. I adore you both dearly. **Claire Marriott** – an absolute weapon, a legendary connector of people, and owner of one of the biggest hearts I know. You've kept me laughing through it all, and your friendship is one of the luckiest breaks I've had. Everyone needs a Claire – I'm just glad I've got the original. **Rod Moynihan** – my fellow journeyman, steadfast ally, and one of the few brave souls willing to stick by me through every twist and turn of this adventure. Thanks for sharing the ride, mate – it's been infinitely better (and far less lonely) having you along. **Jonathon Morse** – mate, you single-handedly gave me the courage to take the leap and start Humanly Agile. You're unquestionably Australia's finest talent whisperer, the Jedi of executive search, and the person I'd call first if I ever misplaced a CEO. I couldn't have done it without your relentless support, insight, and friendship.

My daily circus is held together by a troupe of remarkable colleagues and supporters. **Joshua Clarkson**, whose loyalty and commitment are unmatched, and deserves a medal for enduring my daily craziness. **Pamela Ellis**, my Ambassador of Kwan and gatekeeper extraordinaire – you are quite simply the best assistant anyone could ever dream of. **Ashan Ponnusamy**, my friend and confidant – without our countless lunches, I'd have long ago spiralled into madness. To **Peter Ryan** – the ultimate stealth closer of deals, and the man who taught me how to survive (mostly intact) inside the belly of a Big Four firm. Your lessons on navigating partnership bullshit, dodging pointless meetings, and mastering the art of understatement deserve their own survival manual. Quietly effective, endlessly patient, and never one to brag – you've probably closed another deal just reading this. **Ian McCall**, my Jedi Master, you are the number one strategy consultant in the country and the first call I make whenever I inevitably find myself in a mess. **John Meacock**, I am lucky to count you as a friend; your sage advice has certainly smoothed off many of my rough edges. **David Cooper**, the master of deals and the drinker of red – thank you for always answering my calls when I'm way out of my depth. **Chris Wilson**, growth master, founder whisperer, and trusted Negroni conspirator – thank you for your unwavering friendship and impeccable taste in cocktails. To my co-founders at Impacted – **Karen**, **Anna**, and **Julian**, your endless energy keeps me both in the game and on my toes. **Jack Karikas**, **David Lewis** and **Mike Smith** at Mentorlist – your steady stream of ideas, inspiration, and discussions with Australia's greatest leaders has been amazing.

I am indebted to the clients who trusted me before it was fashionable. **Don Wright** – mate, where do I even start? Serving as Chief Entrepreneur in Residence at Western Sydney University has been one of the greatest privileges of my life. Your understated yet impactful work transforming the innovation ecosystem at WSU epitomises the spirit of Western Sydney – just quietly getting shit done. **Kenan Hibberd** at Unitywater, you backed me from the outset, and it's been an honour to help bring your vision to life. To the phenomenal team at KPMG Futures – **Sarah Vega**, **James Mabbott**, **Tim Winzar**, **Petah Marian**, and **Michelle Carter** – you continue to inspire me every day and your contributions to the Australian startup ecosystem are truly remarkable. A special shout-out to **Emilie Werrin**, who reignited my spark, reminded me that laughter and consulting are not mutually exclusive, and remains one of the best management consultants I've had the pleasure to work with. The team at KPMG US & Global, led by my partner in crime, **Cliff Justice** (alongside **Becky**, **Anuj**, and **Vivek**) – your groundbreaking work in innovation continually sets new standards. To **David Rowlands**, Global Head of AI at KPMG International, your steadfast support and collaboration have been instrumental.

Finally, a salute to the professionals who keep the lights on and the wheels turning. **Michael Hanrahan** at Publish Central shepherded this manuscript from half-baked idea to printed reality. **Peter Hodges**, who in my humble opinion is the best commercial lawyer in Australia – thanks for saving me from myself more times than I care to admit. **Jonathan Isman**, my master of coin and ever-patient accountant – thank you for dealing with my annual financial chaos. **Jesse**, my personal trainer, who bravely attempts to keep my body running despite my stubborn insistence on treating it more like an amusement park than a temple. The design magicians at **Ink & Iris** turned my ramblings into a cover that even my mum wants to frame. And **Fiona Shand** – confidant, friend and occasional gravity check – makes sure my feet touch the ground often enough that I don't float away entirely.

Writing a book takes a village, and I am immensely grateful to have the best village anyone could ask for.

Step Into the Lab – Your Next Bold Move

The last page of a book is only the first page of what you build next. Scan the QR code or visit **dreamstreamlabs.com** and drop straight into DreamStream Labs, our free founder community where the Blueprint turns into traction.

- **Direct access to me and a cohort of battle-tested founders:** Pressure-test ideas, unblock obstacles and celebrate wins in real time.
- **Downloadable templates, canvases and cheat-sheets:** Lift the best bits from these pages and apply them to your venture without reinventing the wheel.
- **Mini-courses and live clinics:** Deep-dive on blind validation, rapid prototyping and AI accelerators – because theory without practice is just fuel still in the drum.
- **Accountability sprints:** Weekly check-ins keep you shipping, iterating and out of the failure swamp.
- **Early-bird access to new tools and events:** Be first in line for beta features, workshops and founder retreats before they hit the wider world.

No paywalls. No vanity metrics. Just a curated space where desire, value and urgency collide – exactly as the DreamStream Blueprint demands.

Ready?

Scan, join, and let's turn ideas into impact – together.

www.ingramcontent.com/pod-product-compliance
Lightning Source LLC
Chambersburg PA
CBHW040920210326
41597CB00030B/5140